"In a witty, conversational series of twelve lessons, Susan teaches us how to learn from our mistakes so we can be more successful the next time. If you are a woman in business, the biggest mistake you can make is to not read this book. It's an empowering must-read for entrepreneurs."

—Ellen Fisher, publisher, Women's Yellow Pages

"Susan Spencer's unique career path gives her insight into the worlds of business and leadership, which she expertly shares in *Briefcase Essentials*. This book should have a permanent place on every businesswoman's bookshelf."

—Susan Gunelius, author of *30-Minute Social Media Marketing* and *Blogging All-in-One for Dummies*, owner of WomenOnBusiness.com, and president/CEO of KeySplash Creative, Inc.

"Women executives at every stage of their career will discover many highly effective tools and strategies for success in business in *Briefcase Essentials*. I have utilized almost all of Susan Spencer's recommended tools in my forty-five years of building a highly successful weight-management business."

—Marilyn Price Birnhak, founder/president, Weight Watchers of Philadelphia

"I've spent over twenty years in the oldest boys club there is: Wall Street. Susan Spencer's book gives you the keys to not only unlocking the old boys network but also to competing and getting ahead just like she did in the NFL and beyond."

—Richard Reyle, partner and senior vice president of a wealth management team at Merrill Lynch

"An interesting account of one woman's journey to business success in a man's world. Susan Spencer clearly explains how a woman's basic instincts and multitasking abilities can be utilized in the competitive world of business. An easy read well worth the time."

—Lorraine Hunt Bono, former lieutenant governor of Nevada

"Susan Spencer's book gets what too many business books miss: Women have innate talents and abilities that can give them an edge in the business world. Spencer uses her expert storytelling skills to show entrepreneurs how they can use her '12 business essentials' to achieve the success they dream of. This book is a must-read for all women business owners!"

—Barbara Corcoran, founder, The Corcoran Group

"If you think every woman going into business should read *Briefcase Essentials*, you are smart. If you think any woman currently in the business world should definitely read the book, you're not only smart, you're intelligent. If you think that any man, whether in business or not, should treat this book as required reading, you're not only intelligent, you're brilliant. *Briefcase Essentials* is the clearest guide to how intelligent women think that I have ever read. Every man should read it."

—Thom Mayer, MD, medical director, NFL Players Association, and founder/chairman of the board, BestPractices, Inc.

BRIEFCASE ESSENTIALS

BRIEFCASE ESSENTIALS

DISCOVER YOUR 12 NATURAL TALENTS

for ACHIEVING SUCCESS *in a*

MALE-DOMINATED WORKPLACE

Susan T. Spencer

GREENLEAF
BOOK GROUP PRESS

This publication is designed to provide accurate and authoritative information in regard to the subject matter covered. It is sold with the understanding that the publisher and author are not engaged in rendering legal, accounting, or other professional services. If legal advice or other expert assistance is required, the services of a competent professional should be sought.

Published by Greenleaf Book Group Press
Austin, Texas
www.gbgpress.com

Distributed by Greenleaf Book Group LLC

For ordering information or special discounts for bulk purchases, please contact Greenleaf Book Group LLC at PO Box 91869, Austin, TX 8709, 512.891.6100.

Cover design by Greenleaf Book Group LLC
Design and composition by Greenleaf Book Group LLC and
Publications Development Company

Publisher's Cataloging-In-Publication Data
(Prepared by The Donohue Group, Inc.)
Spencer, Susan T.
    Briefcase essentials : discover your 12 natural talents for achieving success in a male-dominated workplace / Susan T. Spencer.— 1st ed.
    p. ; cm.
    ISBN: 978-1-60832-080-6
    1. Spencer, Susan T. 2. Businesswomen—Anecdotes. 3. Success in business—Anecdotes. 4. Women—Life skills guides. I. Title.
HD6054 .S64 2011
650.1082   2010935066

Part of the Tree Neutral® program, which offsets the number of trees consumed in the production and printing of this book by taking proactive steps, such as planting trees in direct proportion to the number of trees used:
www.treeneutral.com

TreeNeutral

Printed in the United States of America on acid-free paper

10 11 12 13 14 15   10 9 8 7 6 5 4 3 2 1

First Edition

This book is dedicated to the women all over the world who are watching, listening, learning, and sharing their secrets with each other about how to achieve success in business. Change is at our doorstep. Pursuing opportunities to own their own businesses is the surest way for working women to hasten true equality in the workplace.

CONTENTS

ACKNOWLEDGMENTS

First and foremost, my husband, Robert S. Spencer, deserves more appreciation and praise than words can convey. Without his honest advice and wise counsel, this book could not have been written.

I am grateful to my mother, Jayne E. Achter, for her incredible patience and indispensable participation in the book writing process. A special thank-you to my daughter, Marnie Schneider, who showered me with encouragement and insightful feedback.

I thank Sheila Dyan, my editor, whose literary talent is noteworthy and who made invaluable contributions every step of the way. I thank my publicist Stu Coren, of Rosen-Coren, for his wisdom and balance and his cheerleading as well.

I also thank my family and friends who read various versions of the book as it developed and gave me the benefit of their time and meaningful observations.

BRIEFCASE
ESSENTIALS

INTRODUCTION

A Tale of Two Tonys

Whomp!

Tough Tony Ferrari sank down in his chair and his arms flew up in self-defense as I smacked him on the top of his head with a history book . . . a *big* history book. Before he or I could say a word . . . *Brrrinnnng!*

We were saved by the bell—literally. Tony stood up, sashayed from his desk to the door, ahead of the rest of the class, and flipped me the bird as he left the classroom. It was 1966, a year I'll always remember, because my bout with Tony Ferrari opened my eyes to the unique way women can take over a situation and become successful—in other words, *lead*—in the predominantly male world of business.

What I could never have imagined then was that in the ten years thereafter I'd earn a degree in law and find myself dealing with a whole team of tough guys—as vice president, legal counsel, and acting general manager of the Philadelphia Eagles football team—and well on my way to understanding that women run businesses differently from the way men do.

I guess all of this needs a bit of explaining, which is why I wrote this book—to clarify for myself and to open your eyes to the natural ability of women to practice business in ways that give them a decisive edge.

Let me back up a bit and start from the beginning. I attended Boston University, where I pursued a liberal arts degree with a minor in education. My final semester I worked as a teacher's aide in an upscale neighborhood in the Boston suburbs. Although I thought of teaching as rewarding work, I was undoubtedly influenced by my mother's constant refrain, "Susan, don't forget, you can always get a job as a teacher." If my mother had urged me to be a lawyer, I probably would have headed in that direction sooner, but female lawyers were few and far between in the 1960s.

My first full-time teaching job was as a geography teacher in East Meadow Junior High on Long Island, New York, in the fall of 1962, just after I graduated. The school was in a middle-class neighborhood, and the student body was a cross section of high achievers to borderline dropouts. My classes ran the gamut. When I was hired, the superintendent of the school district said to me, "I promise you that in your first year here you will learn a lot more than your students do." He was so right.

Teaching New York state geography, I barely kept a step ahead of my students. I still remember some of my honors students asking me zingers—questions I couldn't answer until I went home and did some research. I'd level with them when I couldn't answer a question, and I discovered that telling them the truth was the quickest and surest way to gain their respect.

Women are different from men in this regard: the female ego does not get in the way of truth telling. Women are usually more straightforward and candid than men are when answering questions. These qualities help women gain respect and credibility in business.

I loved my work and looked forward to every day—that is, until my fourth year, when I noticed a major change in the atmosphere at the school. It was also when disciplinary procedures changed. During my first three years at East Meadow Junior High, the principal handled all disciplinary problems. (Although in my case, I never needed to send anyone to the principal's office.) At the beginning of my fourth year, however, teachers were told to handle disruptive students on their own. This was a different ball game, and things quickly got out of hand throughout the school.

One of my classes was especially difficult because of one student (as I mentioned earlier). Tough Tony—aptly named by his classmates—was two years older than his classmates because he had been left back twice. He was not only loud and boisterous but also big and strong, and he used his age and size to bully his classmates . . . girls as well as boys. I was a strong teacher, but I knew that physically I was no match for Tony. I also knew he had a short fuse, and I became concerned that if Tony lost it, I'd have to step in to handle the situation.

I talked to the principal, Mr. Bryant, about Tony and the way he'd taken over the class. When I asked for his advice, he said to me: "Susan, I have enough problems. You've been here long enough to handle it yourself." Mr. Bryant had obviously delegated the problem solving to me.

One day, about six weeks into the school year, Tony came up to the front of the class without warning and began shouting a string of the foulest four-letter words I had ever heard— and some in Italian that I'd never heard. I knew that if I didn't discipline him, the class would know *he* was in control, not me, and I'd lose every ounce of credibility I had with them. With only seconds to react, I picked up the biggest book on my desk and chased him back to his desk. Once he was seated, I took the book in both hands and *Whomp!*

So now you know how Tough Tony came to be the target of my history book . . . and I the target of his rude parting gesture. (I apologized later to the principal for my unfortunate use of that book, by the way, and admitted it hadn't been the best way to handle the situation.) Here's the rest of the story, and what I learned from it.

For the next several days, Tony was not in school, and his classmates eagerly participated in class during his absence. I quickly realized that as long as Tony was in my class, the rest of the students would suffer.

Toward the end of the week, I left school feeling frustrated and sad at the prospect of wasting time keeping order while being prevented from teaching students who really wanted to learn. When I got home, I fell despondently into a chair and thought back to the events of the last day Tony was in class. That's when I remembered the note. Two girls had come up at the end of class and left a tightly folded sheet of paper on my desk, which I'd thrown into my purse without reading. I retrieved the note and was surprised to find that, as I opened it, my hands were trembling. The note simply said, "Tony is bad."

I returned to school the next morning determined to take on the principal—and the superintendent, if necessary—to get Tony out of my class. I was prepared to quit or get fired if the school did not see it my way. As I walked toward my classroom, Mr. Bryant's secretary motioned for me to follow her down the corridor to his office, where Mr. Bryant asked me to sit down and tell him what had happened with Tony Ferrari. When I finished giving him the details, I asked if Tony was hurt. Mr. Bryant replied: "Only enough to complain to his father about being hit. They'll be meeting with us here shortly."

Then the principal told me that Tony's father was an influential, well-connected contractor who had built many commercial buildings in the area. He was outraged that one of his son's teachers had hit him and was thinking about pressing charges for assault and battery.

A few minutes later, the secretary announced that Tony senior and Tony junior were waiting impatiently in the front office. As Mr. Bryant told her to escort them to his office, I sensed from his body language that he was going to leave the battle in my hands. But I knew that, although I was a mere five feet, four inches tall, and weighed just 110 pounds, I could hold my own, if our sparring was limited to words.

The two Tonys strode into the office. Tony senior looked angry and eager to defend his son's honor. His eyes quickly darted from the principal to me and then landed on his son . . . and he laughed, long and hard. "*This* is the teacher who hit you?" he asked.

Tony junior's eyes were glued to his feet as he shook his head yes, whereupon his father grabbed him by the back of his collar and pushed him against the wall, all the while spewing a stream of Italian words that I'm sure I'd heard from Tony junior in my classroom a few days before. Tony senior told him to look me straight in the eye and start apologizing.

At first Tony junior only managed a quiet, "I'm sorry," but Tony senior threatened, "You can do better than that— *much* better!"

After Tony junior mumbled a few more words of apology, I turned to his father and told him that as long as we had an understanding that Junior would no longer curse or cause a distraction of any kind, he could return to my class. Tony senior thanked me over and over and gave me his private phone number to use if I ever needed to reach him. He assured me, though, that his son had gotten the message.

Clearly, being a woman saved me that day. What wasn't clear to me was *how*, but I sensed it had something to do with the instant rapport established between Tony senior and me. Tough Tony's father smiled broadly when I walked across the room and extended my hand and said "Good-bye." It was a reach that felt easy, and comfortable. I couldn't identify it then, but now I know that *engagement* and *perceptive communication* are two of the proven business talents (described in chapters 4 and 10) that give women positive results in business.

By the way, Tough Tony apparently did get his father's message. At the end of that school year, he was finally promoted to eighth grade!

CHAPTER 1

Tennis Anyone?

In 1969, when I was twenty-seven years old, I divorced my first husband and moved with my two-year-old daughter to south Florida.

This was not the first time I had started a new life in Florida. Sixteen years earlier, my mother, who was newly divorced, my sister, and I moved from a large, fancy house in the rolling hills of suburban Philadelphia to a small apartment in Miami Beach.

We settled into a quiet but good life, and the years passed quickly.

Fortunately, while my ex-husband and I had been married, we lived with my in-laws, and during that time I was able to save about $25,000 from my teacher's salary for a rainy day, which came sooner than I expected.

So there I was, starting over again in Florida, only this time as a single mom. My mom had remarried and moved back to Philadelphia, but remembering how much I loved the year-round sunny climate as I was growing up, I thought it would be a great place to raise my daughter.

Within a few days of arriving in Fort Lauderdale, I rented a cute two-bedroom house. The first thing I did was buy a roller and several buckets of the whitest paint I could find, and, over the next three weeks, I repainted the entire house myself. I didn't realize it at the time, but I now understand this was my way of taking control of my life.

I lived frugally the first year on my modest income as a part-time substitute teacher, but I soon found it to be unsatisfying; teaching was becoming less of a joy and more of a chore. I had to find something else to do. I just didn't know what.

Finding My Way . . . on the Tennis Court

Playing tennis on the weekends was my only opportunity to get real exercise, and it was a great way to meet people. But as much as I loved playing tennis, that's how much I hated wearing the tennis outfits being sold in the '60s: short, straight-cut dresses designed for women with what I call a French body—no breasts, no hips, no butt, and stick legs. My figure was more Rubenesque—rounded, with generous hips, a healthy pair of thighs, and a noticeable butt.

I couldn't stand looking at myself in the mirror in one of those dresses, which accentuated all my more-than-voluptuous features, and I decided to do something about it. I designed

some tennis dresses to fit my body type and had Bea, an altera-
tions lady I knew, sew them. Flaring out at the waist, ample
in the bust, and slightly longer than other tennis dresses, they
covered all my curves, plus, they had pockets, so I didn't have to
stuff an extra tennis ball up into my underwear.

Starting a business was the last thing on my mind, but my
newfound tennis friends pushed me into it.

"I absolutely love that dress!" said one. "Where did you
buy it?"

"I had it made for me," I replied.

"Can I have one made for me too?"

"Of course," I said, even before asking Bea, being eager
to please.

One thing led to another, and one dress led to another, and
within a few weeks, Bea had sewn six more dresses for my new
best friends. When I saw that they cost me more to make than
I could charge for them—yet still more friends were clamoring
for them—I reached for the Yellow Pages to find a manufacturer
to produce my designs on a larger scale. It was becoming clear
that I could sell the dresses not only to my friends but also to
any tennis player with my zaftig build and access to a pro shop.

After numerous dead-end calls with people who spoke only
Spanish or who hung up on me before I'd finished my whole
spiel, I found myself on the phone with Izzie, a Russian immi-
grant who spoke with a thick accent. Although it was difficult
to understand much of what he said, his sincerity and decency
came through loud and clear. Women have a distinct advantage
because they are able to comprehend a person's nature—even
when the communication is telephone talk.

It's important to note the place of the telephone in business, and the advantage a woman can have using this mode of communication with male colleagues. Simply the fact that the voice on the phone is feminine can create immediate interest for a man on the other end of the line.

It's all about the fantasy—how the man imagines the woman. I've found that projecting an upbeat, confident, and outgoing personality over the telephone is an effective means of communicating that women need to put into practice.

Always remember that the best way to communicate is in person, and the next best way is on the telephone. All other means (especially e-mail and text messages) are impersonal and will not give you the opportunity to have a personal, two-way connection. By talking to the other person, you will have a chance to ask questions and reveal part of your personality; likewise, you have a chance to observe the tone, choice of words, inflection, and even the subtle auditory cues from the other person that you pick up during a telephone conversation.

Those "subtle auditory cues," as suggested by the celebrated anthropologist Helen Fisher in her book *The First Sex*,[1] will help you replay what you heard "mentally" and help give you "cues to size others up."[2] Most of the business I've conducted over twenty years has been via the telephone with men I've never met.

Getting back to my first contact with Izzie, despite my not even being in business yet, he said, "Susan, why don't you visit my factory so that we can talk some more?"

The enthusiasm I projected on that first phone call was genuine. The very next day I went to his factory in the garment district of downtown Miami.

Izzie was warm and welcoming when we met, and I felt an instant connection to this old-world Russian gentleman. I'd say he truly liked women and appeared to be immediately comfortable with me. Women have an uncanny talent for sizing up other people. Fisher describes this as "mind reading."[3]

I instinctively knew that Izzie would open up to me and brag to me about his accomplishments. I listened patiently to his stories and praised him for his successes, understanding that we were building a relationship . . . and that business is built on relationships.

After a long, fascinating conversation about his beloved Russia, as well as the hardships his family had endured after World War II, Izzie and I got down to the business of tennis dresses.

I showed him the handmade garments my dressmaker had put together and asked him a lot of questions about how to go about making them on a larger scale. I was delighted to see that Izzie was taking me seriously, carefully answering my questions, making sure I understood everything he said. He was *helping* me.

He sent me off with the names of several local fabric manufacturers and an assignment: "Find a good pattern maker and come back to me with a professionally made sample dress."

I left Izzie's factory that day filled with a sense of possibility I had never before experienced. Driving home, I realized that I actually could start my own business, be my own boss, make all the decisions, as long as I was able to ask for and accept help.

BE #1 BEING ABLE TO ASK FOR HELP

Help is defined as providing assistance, advice, or other information. Even though Izzie was a complete stranger, my straightforward and earnest approach of asking a number of intelligent questions convinced him that I was determined to start a business and that I needed his guidance to move the process along. Asking Izzie for **help** that first day we met became the foundation of a practice I followed thereafter.

In researching her book *How She Does It*, Margaret Heffernan talked to hundreds of business owners across the country and identified "asking for help" as one of the "common attitudes" that women share.[4] Margaret concludes that "asking for help is a sign of strength," and adds the following advice: "If you can't accept help, your business will never be smarter than you are."[5]

Persistence Pays Off

My search for a pattern maker turned out to be a bit more difficult. By 1968, pattern making had become a lost art in America, and independent pattern makers were hard to find.

After being turned down by the leads Izzie had given me, I spent two weeks calling every clothing manufacturer in Dade County. Finally, after practically begging one of the last clothing manufacturers that actually bothered to come to the phone, I was reluctantly given the name and home phone number of a pattern maker in Fort Lauderdale who had retired a few years earlier due to serious illness. The woman who gave me his number abruptly said to me, "I think he may be dead."

So it was that when I first reached Aaron, I was relieved someone had at least answered the phone; then, after hearing his gruff, mumbled greeting, I wasn't so sure. He sounded old and crotchety, like he didn't want to be bothered. But he was my only hope, so I ignored his response, which felt as if he had slammed the door in my face.

"Aaron," I said, "I met with the owner of a large clothing manufacturer in Miami who told me I needed to find a good pattern maker, so I called you."

"I'm retired and not well. I'm not interested," he replied.

I would have started begging, but before I did, I surprised myself by blurting out, "Can I visit you at your home?"

"*No!*" said Aaron.

Then I started begging, and crying was not far behind. "Aaron, I just need you to get me started; it won't take much time, please," I said. "*Please* can I make a short visit?"

When he practically whispered yes, I cheerfully said, "Great, I'll see you tomorrow."

Then I asked for his address and hung up before he could change his mind.

The next day, when Aaron opened the door, I greeted him with a small basket of fruit, which I held onto because I saw Aaron was in a wheelchair with a colostomy bag hanging from it.

Walking into his little apartment, I started to talk business . . . and never asked him about his medical condition. If he could make my patterns, that was good enough for me.

After a minute or two, he started to talk to me. And the more we talked, the more he relaxed and showed me who he really was—a very lonely man.

His memory was incredible as he related his history as a pattern maker, starting as an apprentice in Brooklyn in 1915. Although he was humble about his accomplishments, he'd worked for some of the biggest names in the industry, designing everything from sports clothing to ballroom gowns.

I felt a little embarrassed to show him my sample, afraid he'd brush it off as amateurish, but when I handed it to him, he looked it over with a critical eye. For what seemed like a lifetime, he said nothing, letting out only a few grunts.

Getting anxious, I was about to press him for a word—any word. Before I could say a thing, he said, "I will commit to make two basic patterns for you."

"Good! Let's get started next week," I said.

Being persistent had paid off.

BE #2 BEING PERSISTENT

Persistence (which, contrary to some men's interpretation, is not to be confused with *nagging* or *stubbornness*) is the ability to focus on the job that needs to be accomplished, combined with the stick-to-itiveness to see it through to completion. Persistence is a trait that women share in common and one that is indispensable if you want to succeed in business.

In *Through the Labyrinth*, authors Alice E. Eagly and Linda L. Carli identify strength, skill, and persistence—citing case studies and personal anecdotes—as the qualities women need to move up the corporate ladder in a "highly male-dominated hierarchy."[6]

• • •

Because I was persistent, I was able to overcome several obstacles in order to identify, locate, and hire a talented craftsman who performed a critical task for my fledgling company. **Being persistent** throughout my business career enabled me to set short-term goals and accomplish them—two essential prerequisites for business success.

I also learned a valuable business lesson from both Izzie and Aaron about asking for and getting help: there is always a *quid pro quo* (one thing in return for another). Once you receive help in business, you have an obligation to reciprocate. Not surprisingly, reciprocity is another way of showing respect—which women instinctively practice. This was easy with Izzie, as he and I each benefited from the thousands of dresses he manufactured for me. We also enjoyed a great working relationship and friendship.

The *quid pro quo* with Aaron was a bit more complicated. Although he had made only two patterns for me, they turned out to be the heart of my business because they fit many body types. How could I have even begun to repay him? The answer surprised me.

Aaron's apartment wasn't big enough in which to do all the drafting necessary to make my patterns, so he occasionally worked at my house, even though I now realize it must have been a struggle for him to get there. It was apparent he was failing, and I treated him with the compassion and respect I'd shown my grandfather. He'd appear sad and frail when he arrived at my front door; looking back, I remember that he always left smiling and in good spirits, perhaps proud to be working again at something he loved.

In the end, having no idea what it must have cost this ill man in precious time and effort to make my two patterns, I merely said, "Thank you," as I paid him, barely giving a thought to how much he had *helped* me . . . and not understanding at all how much I had *helped* him.

CHAPTER 2

Papillon Spreads Its Wings

In the fall of 1969, with the help of Izzie and Aaron, Papillon tennis dresses were born. The logo was a small white butterfly outlined in blue, with a red tennis racket inside each wing. Izzie agreed to make four production samples from my designs, using the first pattern Aaron had made for me. A few months before Christmas, I called the sportswear department of the Saks Fifth Avenue purchasing office in New York to see if I could show them my dresses.

Although this was a gutsy move for someone with such a small line and no track record in the business, it seemed to me that the quickest way to find out if I had something unique was to show the tennis dresses to one of the most prestigious and well-known department stores in the country. I thought, *Why not? What do I have to lose?* Inquiring would be a surefire way to get an answer.

My first surprise was that the buyer came to the phone. A bigger surprise was that he agreed to see me the following week.

When I arrived for the meeting in New York, I was told to set up in a dressing room in the back of the sportswear department. Most sportswear lines typically have about a hundred pieces and take an hour to arrange. Arranging my *four* tennis dresses took less than a minute.

My appointment was at 4:00 PM. By 5:15 I was still waiting for the buyer and was beginning to think he had heard about my piddling line and was going to cancel the appointment. At 5:30, however, the buyer strolled into the dressing room. Without any introduction, he walked over to the four dresses hanging on a long silver rack.

"Where's the rest of your line?" he asked.

"This is it," I said, hoping he wouldn't laugh and walk out.

He didn't laugh. He didn't walk out. But, for the next ten minutes, he looked critically at my dresses, one at a time.

I didn't need to point out the fine workmanship, as I saw the buyer nod slightly as he turned each dress inside out, seeming to approve of the neat, unusually wide seams not often seen in garments anymore.

Just when I thought the buyer had finished his inspection, he went over the selection again, lingering on one in particular—a white dress with a large rhinestone butterfly on the front. Finally, he turned to me.

"Can you produce five hundred of this one and ship them to me in New York by the first of November?" he asked.

"Certainly!" I said, having no idea if Izzie could deliver.

I soon found out there was no question that Izzie could handle the order. In fact, because his normal production runs were between three thousand and five thousand pieces, he was hesitant to take on such a small order. But when I told him it was for Saks, he got very excited and agreed to make an exception.

The dresses not only sold out that Christmas, the label caught on, and Papillon tennis dresses soon became popular. I expanded the line to a dozen styles, which were sold in department stores and tennis shops all over the country. For the next two years I ran a successful business, but . . . it didn't last.

Know Thyself . . . and Thy Partner

In the third year, I took on a fifty-fifty partner when he invested $500,000 in the company.

Carl and I had gone to high school together, but I barely knew him. Tracking me down at a sports trade show, he showed me his company's tennis dresses and said he was tired of working for a large conglomerate and was ready to make a move. Making him a partner seemed like a good idea at the time.

When he insisted that he be named president of the company, I should have surmised that he would be a real pain to deal with, but a half-million-dollar investment was nothing to sneeze at. I thought I could control him because I was the CEO and chairman of the board and had the exclusive right to hire and fire. I was right about him being a real pain, but wrong about being able to control his actions.

During the first six months we were together, I had just finished a new line called "the sherbets," so named because the dresses were trimmed in lemon, lime, orange, or raspberry terry cloth.

"This is the greatest tennis line I have ever handled," said Carl.

"Carl, remember, we only have a million-dollar line of credit to buy material and pay for manufacturing our dresses, so don't go crazy selling everyone," I warned him sternly.

"I'm president and I'll do what I want. What do *you* know?" Carl shouted back, sarcasm dripping from every word.

When orders started pouring in from all over the country, I called Carl every day, saying, "Stop selling . . . come off the road."

But he continued to sell the line for several more months, taking orders for millions of dollars worth of dresses that we'd never be able to afford to make.

After nine months, I knew there was only one way I could get him off the road and away from potential customers. I called Carl and resolutely exclaimed, "You're fired!"

Unfortunately, we ended up in a lawsuit. I was stuck with the bank loans (because I had failed to get him to sign on personally) and the inventory (hundreds of tennis dresses hanging in my garage). The only way to resolve the stalemate was to dissolve the company. A disastrous result!

For the next two years, I spent six days a week collecting Papillon's receivables and selling off the inventory so that I could pay down the bank debt. That left me with nothing monetarily to show for all that effort and success. But by keeping a positive outlook toward future business opportunities, I was **adapting** to my new reality and managed to give it an optimistic spin by knowing that at least I salvaged my reputation with the bankers and could borrow again another day.

BE #3 BEING ADAPTABLE

Being adaptable is defined as the ability to adjust easily to different conditions; finding alternative solutions or new strategies. In fact, a recent book, *How Remarkable Women Lead*, urges women in both work and life to "make adaptability your skill," and "stay adaptive."[1]

When my partner refused to stop taking orders, even though our company had already used up its line of credit, I had very few options—none of them good ones. The more orders he took that could not be filled, the more far-reaching his actions would adversely influence the reputation of our company. It is common knowledge in the garment business that once you take an order from a large department store and fail to deliver it, you have effectively *burned your bridges*. Since my partner would not stop taking orders, firing him seemed like the best solution—in other words, an alternative solution to an impossible situation. My actions stopped him from doing any further damage to our reputation.

That same year, I met another sporting goods salesman at another trade show . . . and married him six weeks later. This was apparently my year for a crash course on partners. I learned the hard way that you never know the skills and personality of others until you partner with them. That's when all the warts come out—in business and in love—and then it's too late. I vividly remember a phone call I made to my sister just a week after Jason and I married. "Why did I marry a man I don't know?!" I cried.

CHAPTER 3

The Eagles Have Landed . . . at My Feet

My husband, daughter, and I moved to Philadelphia in 1976 so Jason could cover a new sales territory, and I, at thirty-five years old, entered Villanova Law School. The acrimonious lawsuit that terminated Papillon taught me a valuable lesson—there are consequences when you sign a contract. I did not go to law school to practice law; rather, I wanted to be armed with legal knowledge to protect myself in future business dealings and avoid the pitfalls that tripped me up in my first business venture.

By 1984, I was the vice president, legal counsel, and acting general manager of the Philadelphia Eagles. (Yes, it's an unlikely job for a woman, and to this day, I remain the only woman in National Football League history to have held all these positions.)

No doubt you're wondering, How did she get *that* job?!

Well, I could tell you I was in the right place at the right time, or I could tell you I was a lawyer and taught myself how to negotiate players' contracts. I could also tell you that football was in my blood from an early age and that I grew up watching famous college coaches of the past, who were frequent guests at our home and drew up plays in our living room. Or I could tell you the *whole* truth: my father owned the team.

When Leonard Tose bought the Eagles in 1969, the National and American football leagues hadn't yet merged, and professional sports, in general, hadn't become the business colossus it is today. But my father was a visionary. He understood that football was great entertainment and could foresee the huge financial windfall that owning a professional football team would bring him.

My dad's management style was straight out of a businessman's playbook: top down all the way. To handle the day-to-day decisions, he hired a general manager, who in turn hired his friends to make up the rest of Eagles management. None of these men had experience managing a sports team—or any business, for that matter.

Added to this woeful lack of experience was my father's penchant for the extravagant. Notoriously flamboyant, dashing, and a real folk hero in Philadelphia, my father lived in a mansion and was chauffeured around town in his Rolls-Royce. He frequently had a glamorous woman on his arm and trumpeted his arrival at every home football game by landing at the stadium in his helicopter (its side emblazoned with a giant green eagle).

My father's venture into the world of sports fit right in with this lifestyle—full of excitement, bravado, and gambling—a lifestyle supported by large sums borrowed from banks, based on the increasing value of the team. By the time I arrived on the scene, the Eagles owed millions of dollars. Women have a different view about the benefits of owning or running a profitable company. For them, it's about "growing reputation, credibility, and reliability."[1] Rather than use profits to support a lavish lifestyle, women put profits back into their companies to fund innovation, pay off debts, and share success with employees—to ensure that the business survives over the long term.[2]

I began working part-time with the Eagles organization at the end of my second year of law school. A high-priced Philadelphia law firm was handling the team's legal work, but the majority of that paperwork pertained to routine contract matters and basic employee-related issues. So I convinced my father he could save money by hiring me as the team's in-house legal department (and I could make a little money to help pay for law school).

As "legal consultant" for the team—with a year of law school still left to complete—I began quietly looking into the team's contracts and financial records, quickly discovering that the Eagles franchise was being spent into bankruptcy. In hindsight, the fact that my inquiring didn't raise concern among management is in itself curious; this is not surprising, however, as many men have a tendency to underestimate a woman's intelligence and comprehension of business issues.

The unemotional and almost distant attitude I adopted in the beginning worked to my advantage during my first year with the Eagles: it allowed me to research under the radar and gain valuable knowledge without confrontation.

Over the next two years, after graduating law school, I continually brought examples of questionable expenses to my dad's attention. Each time I appeared with another instance, he just shook his head, but he said nothing. I didn't think he took my show and tell seriously, but one day, out of the blue, he surprised everyone. He called the general manager into his office and, without any discussion, said, "Johnny, you're fired."

He then called me in and said, "Susan, I just fired Johnny; you fire the rest of his team."

I knew at that moment that this old-style businessman had just moved me to second in command!

So there I was, the acting GM of the Philadelphia Eagles and running the day-to-day team business. My position was never made public, however, and would never be made official because my father wasn't comfortable having a woman at the helm. To him, and many men of his generation, women belonged at home taking care of the house and children.

So why did he hire me? Because I was already working at the Eagles and had demonstrated competence and credibility over the previous three years. And, all else being equal, family trumps strangers.

My new position gave me a once-in-a-lifetime opportunity to run a multimillion-dollar business and to demonstrate that I could successfully manage the organization as a *businesswoman*, and make the team profitable.

A Spoonful of Sugar

Like my father, the team always traveled in style. When they played on the road, in a city more than a few hours away from Philadelphia by bus—about five times during the regular season—they traveled on a jumbo jet. This luxury plane could fly nonstop from Philadelphia to California and carried not only the coaches and players but also members of the press and numerous friends of friends. Sure, it was nice . . . but it was a huge expense that the Eagles could ill afford.

One of the first financial cuts I made as acting GM was to contract with a smaller regional carrier for a plane whose size would accommodate only team personnel.

Saving money was a new concept to the players, who assumed that sports teams had unlimited budgets when it came to spending money on them. They quickly learned that the "sky" was not the limit and that cutting expenses would become the new norm. They grumbled unhappily as they climbed aboard the small plane for the first time. But their displeasure was nothing compared to my father's.

"You're embarrassing me!" he muttered under his breath as he settled into his seat next to me on the first flight, which was destined for San Diego. I knew there was nothing I could say or do to console him, so I kept my mouth shut, my eyes straight ahead, and waited for the next shoe to drop . . . which it did, a few hours into the flight, when the plane began its descent over North Dakota to refuel.

"What the hell is this?!" my father roared, his outrage echoing among the rest of the passengers.

Once the plane was on the ground, the team was instructed to deplane and wait in the small airport lounge, where they could stretch their legs and make phone calls. Their grumbling leaving the plane was even louder than it had been boarding the plane. I dared not look at my father, whose slow burn was about to explode into a wildfire.

As I left the plane, I didn't head for the lounge but stayed nearby, waiting to pull the rabbit out of my hat: carts filled with large cartons of Baskin-Robbins ice cream, oozing containers of hot fudge, and bowls full of bananas, whipped cream, sprinkles, nuts, and more were wheeled up to the plane's steps. When everyone returned to the plane and saw the sweet extravaganza before them, they started hooting and applauding loudly. Giant scoops of ice cream and toppings were shoveled into large plastic bowls and carried onboard. Fifteen minutes later, the plane took off . . . and everyone was smiling.

If I had told my father or any of the coaches or players that I was going to trade their jumbo jet for a jumbo ice cream sundae, they would have laughed in my face. Nonetheless, by coming up with a novel business **improvisation**, ice cream carts became a stopover tradition, one that everyone—including my father—enjoyed and looked forward to.

Yes, a spoonful of sugar does help the medicine go down, and yes, the way to a man's heart is often through his stomach—old sayings familiar to everyone. But women take them seriously, which is why this creative idea could only have come from a woman. Just ask any man. You'd no doubt find that his sweet solution to the situation might have included something along the lines of lap dancers in fishnet stockings, or maybe he'd just say, "Suck it up and shut up."

BE #4 BEING IMPROVISATIONAL

Women **improvise** in business by coming up with solutions to unexpected challenges. It is important that you appreciate and practice your natural ability to **improvise**, using original and sometimes unconventional ideas, because it will give you an incredible edge and, in some cases, create quite a buzz. Margaret Heffernan offers this advice: "Be a good planner but a brilliant improviser. Success hinges on handling surprises, not denying them."[3]

Not every change I made as acting general manager went over as well. I raised ticket prices for the first time in six years. This was because the team needed to generate more revenue and Philly's ticket prices lagged behind all other large market teams. Naturally, my actions made me very unpopular with many hard-core fans. When I replaced the jumbo jet with a smaller plane, forcing the press to fly commercially, the press took it personally. The final straw was when I substituted hot dogs and Philly cheesesteaks in place of the gourmet lobster and filet mignon lunches that the press had enjoyed for many years on game day at Veteran's Stadium (the Eagles' home field).

The press *rewarded* me with a new title—"The Wicked Witch of the Vet."

Looking back now, it's comical, but at the time, it hurt. My **adaptable** approach (remember BE #3) to handling the press's negative and very personal criticism of me was effortless—I stopped reading the Philly papers!

CHAPTER 4

Presentation, Presentation, Presentation

My dad had a favorite expression that he frequently repeated to me: *Presentation is everything.* This gem of an idea, which I describe as **being engaging,** served me well throughout my career, and I practiced it often during my time with the Eagles. The success of initiating a new business relationship is determined by the impression you make. Your ability to communicate openness and exude self-confidence is crucial . . . and that takes lots of practice.

Meeting and Greeting

Have you observed the way most businessmen greet each other? I have. They immediately extend their hand and wait for the other person to do the same; then they grasp hands firmly and give a shake or two. Generally, they don't make eye contact with each other, and if they exchange words, they're often mumbled and perfunctory.

When women greet each other, they hug, they smile, and they look each other in the eye and say how good it is to see the other one. This is true even if they're business colleagues. These gestures are more than symbolic—it's how women use body language to communicate the importance of relationships.

When you meet a businessperson in the ordinary course of business, practice greeting him or her with an extended hand, and look the person squarely in the eye. Grasp the person's hand firmly, confidently—no dead-fish grip—and clearly introduce yourself, including your name and your title. Ask for the person's name and position, and repeat the name while still making eye contact and before you let go of the other person's hand. **Being engaging** includes the way you meet and greet other businesspersons. It begins the moment you extend your hand and continues throughout the greeting.

BE #5 BEING ENGAGING

Based on my experience, **being engaging**, in a business context, can make the difference between success and failure.
One book has described it as "finding your voice ... standing
up to be counted, choosing to act on opportunities that car-

ry risk, and facing your deep-seated fears."[1] **Being engaging** is a skill that should *not* be taken lightly. In fact, it can be the most powerful Briefcase Essential you carry.

The following anecdote will fill you in on the end of the Eagles story while illustrating that **engaging** is absolutely critical when you initiate a business contact.

I Am My Father's Son

Despite the fact that I managed to get the Eagles' finances under control so that the organization stopped hemorrhaging money, I couldn't significantly reduce the team's debt, which in 1984 was still more than $30 million. When the principal bank notified us that their loan was due to be paid off in less than a year, I tried to find replacement financing. But at every turn, I got the same answer: "Not if your father controls the money."

My dad refused to turn financial control of the team over to me or anyone else. Desperate, he even considered moving the Eagles out of Philadelphia if he could find investors and a bank elsewhere that would loan him money.

When a group in Arizona expressed an interest, I thought moving the team there might be an ideal solution. The organization would receive a lifesaving infusion of money, and my father might tone down his over-the-top lifestyle. But when a vote was taken, the only *yes* vote to move the team was mine.

Nevertheless, my father sent me to meet with the Arizona bankers to see if they'd loan him the money and allow him to continue to hold the purse strings. He believed that if he got the financing he so desperately needed, he'd find a way to justify—to his committee and himself—moving the Eagles to Arizona.

I arrived at the bank, located in a beautiful, modern, southwestern building in downtown Phoenix, and was ushered into the lobby of the executive suite. I signed in at the reception desk and took a seat, then watched the matronly, gray-haired receptionist stand up and check out my name on the sign-in sheet. She stood still for a moment, looking somewhat confused. Then she walked over to me and whispered: "Who are you here to see? Are you waiting for others from the Eagles to join you?"

I told her I'd come alone and that I was scheduled to meet with the four senior lenders of the bank.

"Oh, I see," she said, but she didn't move. She just stood next to me, still appearing to be somewhat perplexed.

"Is there a problem?" I asked.

"Oh no, I'll introduce you in a moment. But ... what is your official title?" she asked.

"Vice president and legal counsel," I replied.

Her eyebrows now noticeably went up, she suddenly stood straighter, and she turned and walked back to her desk. No doubt she wasn't told to expect a woman. *Surprise!* I thought, smiling to myself.

At every initial Eagles business meeting I ever attended alone, most men had the same reaction: *Oh, she's a woman; what can she possibly know about football or business?* By this time, I was used to the reaction and had come prepared.

A few moments later, the doors to the conference room swung open. The receptionist introduced me as I walked into the room and observed four middle-aged men momentarily staring blankly at me. Seated around a long, shiny, mahogany conference table, the men then looked down at the papers before them. Discomfort rose from the group and hit me in the face like steam from a pot of boiling water. Clearly, they weren't expecting a woman.

Unfazed, I walked around the table, looked each banker in the eye as I shook his hand, introduced myself, and smiled. Coming full circle, with all eyes now on me, I said, "I'm sure you didn't expect to meet with a woman, but rest assured, even though I've never played football, I am my father's only son."

After an incredulous moment of silence, all four bankers broke into a hearty, masculine laugh. **Engaging**, by shaking their hands warmly and injecting a little humor, broke the ice. Forty-five minutes later, I had secured a commitment for a loan. I didn't know it at the time, but this was a typical example of how successful businesswomen act.

The situation I faced when I walked into the conference room just described was what I call *the door opener*. Once I entered the banker's inner sanctum, what I said and how I engaged would determine whether I secured a loan commitment or was turned away. A business opportunity commences when you meet someone for the first time. It is within your power to put yourself out there and show others who you are— by **engaging** them. This gives you a decisive edge.

Over the next few weeks, I was able to convince a number of banks in several different cities, some as far away as Vancouver, to refinance the team. The problem was that, like the Philadelphia banks, every one offered the loan with the same strings attached: my father had to agree to give financial control of the team over to someone who was fiscally responsible, assuming I would be an acceptable choice. After all, passing the baton from father to child would be a natural progression in a family business. Ah, but there was the rub! The child in question was not a son: I was my father's *daughter*. In my dad's eyes, having a woman in control of his finances would be an embarrassment, and totally unacceptable.

Bottom line: My father refused to relinquish financial control of the team, and less than a year later, he was forced to sell the franchise.

For me, however, the five years I spent with the Eagles had been a resounding success. I had been given the opportunity—a gift, really—to test running a business by using a woman's Briefcase Essentials rather than doing it *like a man*. By being personally involved in all aspects of the business, I succeeded as a businesswoman in an exclusively male organization. Instead of taking time to have a pity party for myself at having lost the opportunity to continue the family business, I began investigating a new business opportunity.

The fact that it was another all-male industry didn't scare me a bit; perhaps it even intrigued me, because I was beginning to understand the potency of women letting their natural attributes dictate the business rules.

The Tail of the Tale

Not so successful was the management of the man in my personal life. The very exciting years I spent with the Eagles took its toll on my second marriage. My husband hated football as well as the fact that I had such a high-profile job. After seven years together, we mutually agreed it was time to separate and divorce, and once we did, I never looked back.

CHAPTER 5

Out of the Frying Pan, into the Fire

Lifted higher than I could ever have expected to go in the world of business by my experience with the Eagles, I came down from this rarefied air to take stock of my options. I knew I didn't want to practice law, and my gut was telling me I was ready to own my own business and be my own boss again. While continuing to work for the Eagles, I began investigating new business opportunities, eager to see if my business techniques would work when I was on my own and not the boss's daughter.

What some might call downtime—driving time, lunch time, shower time, evening time, weekend time—I, like many women, call *contemplation* minutes—time to explore and think about new possibilities and possible opportunities. Running a business can be a very stressful job, and taking short breaks is how women have learned to naturally reduce tension.[1]

My downtime during this tumultuous period was mostly uptime—in an airplane. For six months, I flew from Philadelphia to Miami, where along with four other attorneys, I worked through complicated and contentious negotiations to hammer out an agreement for the sale of the Eagles. The effort kept me up in the air, both literally and figuratively.

During these final months, I not only worked on the sale of the team but also continued to run the team's business and set up a new office for my dad. It was hectic, hard work, and emotionally draining, but I knew that once this chapter in my life was closed, I'd need to hit the ground running, so I ramped up my research into new opportunities.

In the mid-'80s, it was front-page news in the Philadelphia papers that several casinos—which were licensed by the state—were opening in Atlantic City. My research revealed that state-licensed entities were required by New Jersey state law to award a certain percentage of business contracts to minority-owned businesses. Surprised to learn that *women* were included in the category of *minority*, I called the various state agencies and asked a ton of questions. I concluded that starting a new company to sell a service to the Atlantic City casinos might be an interesting opportunity. The only question remaining was, what service could I offer?

I had worked for my grandfather's trucking company one summer during college, filing bills of lading in the basement of the trucking depot. Meager though it was, this experience in the trucking/delivery business was enough to spark a kernel of an idea: my new woman business enterprise (WBE) would be one that I felt other women would not pursue—a delivery business providing the casinos with whatever they needed to have delivered.

After the idea came more research in the form of talking with buyers at the casinos to learn about their needs. The answer was specialty foods. The larger distributors considered them a nuisance and weren't eager to offer such perishable items because they were small volume items that required special handling.

The more interesting question was, why did these very busy men (and a few women) in a mega-million-dollar industry agree to even talk with someone who was just starting a supply company and had virtually no experience?

My advantage in this case was simply the fact that I was a woman. The buyers agreed to meet with me because, as a WBE, I'd be helping them fulfill their state-licensure obligations. Trust me when I tell you, however, that they were not overly enthusiastic about taking the time to help me.

I listened carefully and patiently to what each buyer told me, and I learned enough to have a sense of what specific food products I could offer that might distinguish me from other distributors.

Another piece of information that resonated with me was that the casinos agreed to pay minority companies quickly. In fact, the terms were "net 10," which meant my invoices would be paid within ten days of the date I delivered the product. This was an incredible advantage because, instead of having to go to a bank and borrow money to cover the cost of paying for goods I bought and would resell, the casinos would pay me twenty days before I needed to turn around and pay my vendors.

I thought back to the cash flow problems I had with Papillon, which eventually sunk my tennis dress business, and said a silent *Hurrah!!* This time, cash flow was a nonissue.

So, in 1986, with $15,000 in the bank, I started Allegro Foods. *Allegro* is Italian for joyous, and that's exactly how it felt to be my own boss again.

A-Tisket, A-Tasket

In the beginning, I sold everything from meat products, to fresh bread, to produce, to fresh-cut flowers. Allegro's special "hook" was offering delivery service twenty-four hours a day, seven days a week.

My first year in business, a buyer from one of the casinos asked if I could provide gift baskets to give to their employees at Christmas. Other distributors weren't anxious to do this, apparently because they felt it required too much dirty work. I took that as an opportunity and agreed to a contract, sure that I'd figure out how to work out the details after the ink was dry.

I located a store that sold baskets from Thailand for just $2 each, bought twenty-five hundred, and filled them with a variety of canned specialty food items I'd like to receive in a gift basket. I also purchased twenty-five hundred frozen turkeys—something I felt every family would appreciate over the holiday season. (Businesswomen often take projects that affect a broad cross section of employees simply because it *feels good*. It's another one of those differences that distinguishes women and men in business.) I hired a few part-time employees to help me put the baskets together in an old warehouse I had rented specifically for the project and got to work.

Having never done this kind of work before, I had no idea what I'd let myself in for. But I soon found out why other vendors—most likely men—didn't fight me for the contract. Instead of taking just a few hours to put the baskets together, the project took more than fourteen hours. It was a long, exhausting day that, at first, gave me second thoughts about my decision to do it. Then I tallied the expenses and income. I had made a profit . . . a huge profit. At $10 net margin per basket, I had made $25,000 in one day!

Along with that profit came the goodwill with the casino, whose employees appreciated the effort their management had made to give them a unique holiday treat.

Within the first few months, I quickly learned which items were carried by large distributors and would not be profitable for my company, and I focused instead on specialty and gourmet food products that had not yet been introduced to the chefs in the Atlantic City casinos. Specialty items, especially meat products, had to be held at a temperature range of 36–42 degrees or they would spoil. Maintaining the correct temperature during delivery required meticulous handling, and therefore these products carried much higher profit margins—that is, the amount you can sell something for minus what it cost you to buy it.

Allegro handled fresh products that took considerable research to find in those days, including handmade sausage, Colorado veal, and organic chicken breasts. I also sold fresh quail I bought from a Pennsylvania Dutch farm I discovered, and wonderful hearth-baked bread that an old-time baker in Philadelphia still made in a brick oven.

After a while, the chefs began asking me to find esoteric items not offered in the traditional marketplace, such as black squid pasta, goat cheese mozzarella, and edible flowers. I'd find the items and then try to get an exclusive to sell them to the casinos. Generally, if I couldn't get an exclusive, I wouldn't handle the product because competition from other distributors would force me to lower my price and I'd lose my profit.

Another key to higher profits was lower expenses. My biggest cost cutter was my decision to run my business without renting a warehouse. "Impossible!" said one distributor, who laughed out loud when he saw my one small refrigerated truck with *Allegro Foods* printed in big red letters on each side.

And that probably was the opinion of the other distributors in Atlantic City, all of whom stored their products in refrigerated warehouses, each managed by several employees.

But it wasn't impossible. I was a practical businesswoman doing what comes naturally—thinking outside the box!

In addition to the rented truck, Allegro Foods had a tiny rented office and two employees: a driver/pickup man and me, which I thought was appropriate for a start-up business.

My driver started at four o'clock every morning to pick up orders from eight or nine suppliers. He'd hustle to load the truck and then drive sixty miles to deliver the fresh food products to five or six casinos that same day.

For the first couple of months, I went with my driver to all the stops to see if any issues arose and to meet the foremen who handled my orders. I did so because, like all successful businesswomen, I believe in practicing direct communication across the board.

Women make it a point to know the names and faces of people they are working with: we want them to know us and we want to feel comfortable with them as well. In some cases, my suppliers felt so comfortable that they shared personal information with me, and our relationship was close enough that I could take concerns or problems directly to them rather than to the owner of the company. This was an advantage because it was the foreman, in fact, who had the ability to solve most problems. I suspect most male managers would have considered this an inappropriate route for the owner of the company, but successful businesswomen are naturally **inclusive** and consistently employ the most effective way to get a job done—by working with employees at all levels.

BE #6 BEING INCLUSIVE

Businesswomen are "people persons." They fill this role naturally because they are comfortable relating one-on-one with people on various levels of an organization; women are inclusive. Businessmen generally tend to act impersonally and do not interact at all levels; they are exclusive. For women, the term "inclusive" carries with it an implicit acknowledgment that "people come first." By **being inclusive** with every business contact—whether customer, supplier, or employee—I discovered that the natural talents women apply to business give them a decisive edge.

My "people come first" approach turned out to be the key to the success of Allegro Foods. Because the employees who worked for my suppliers knew me and appreciated that I took the time to get to know them and listen to them, my orders were always ready and I never had shorts. If a problem arose, one of the foremen would call me before the truck was loaded and we'd quickly work out the issue. In addition, because I took the time to build and nurture these relationships, I earned their loyalty. None of my key suppliers dropped me for a larger, more powerful distributor vying for the business.

A Business Partner You Can Trust—Your Own Instincts

Running Allegro Foods was hardly an easy transition. I went from the posh executive offices of the Eagles, where people were kissing up to me every day—wanting to sit in the owner's box or get close to the players—to being just another food peddler. But being my own boss again and back in the real world of business felt great.

It's critical to understand that starting a business from scratch is a challenge that tests your discipline, fortitude, determination, and sense of self-worth. The first year of my distribution business was physically and mentally exhausting, and I found myself constantly examining my motives and questioning the reasons why I was in this crazy business that I was literally making up as I went along. I always came back to the same answer: I needed to prove to myself that I could create something from nothing and be successful. Trust your instincts that are telling you, *Hang in there, you can do this*, because you can.

Although I knew I didn't want to be in the food distribution business forever, some of the food products I sold interested me, especially the meat products. My instinct told me that by working in my current business another opportunity would come along that would resonate loud and clear. Once again, I listened to my gut—which most authors describe as "intuition"[2]—and moved forward with Allegro Foods. Helen Fisher theorized that women's ability to use their "uniquely constructed and well connected brains" to assimilate a multitude of observations quickly may include "brain-body connections" that allow them to "pick up and assimilate body cues," which, taken together, produce what she describes as "gut thinking."[3]

Larger distributors may have laughed at Allegro, but I had the last laugh—all the way to the bank. It took about a year to iron out the kinks, but by the third year, I grossed $500,000. In fact, I owned Allegro Foods for six years and made a profit *every* year. Not bad for a food peddler without a warehouse.

Music to My Gears—A Truck Driver in Penny Loafers

My success as a distributor didn't come without help ... and help came from an unlikely source. His name was Clem. He was my driver. He was also Donna's ex-husband. Donna was one of the important buyers at Resorts Casino. An aspiring composer with a degree in engineering, Clem had dropped out of several engineering jobs to write music.

One day when I was taking an order from Donna, she asked if I could find a place in my company for her ex-husband, who hadn't made any money in two years.

"What can he do?" I asked her.

"Anything," she said. "What do you need?"

"I need a full-time driver, but I'm not sure that's a suitable job for a songwriter."

"Hire him," she said. "As long as he can take his guitar in the truck and work on his music during downtime, he'll do it."

Clem was a far cry from the stereotypical truck driver. Tall and lanky, with dark wavy hair and a preppy demeanor, Clem insisted on working in well-pressed chinos, a button-down shirt, and penny loafers. I took a flexible and **inclusive**—that is, a businesswoman's approach—to hiring employees, which allowed for distinctive individuals to get a job with my company.[4]

"You look nice, Clem. Too nice for a dirty job like this," I said.

"This is who I am, Susan. I'll be fine," he said.

And he was fine until . . . less than one week later a case of beef fell over, covering Clem in blood.

"Well, you were right about this being a dirty job," he admitted when he called me later that day, "but I'm still me, and I'm not buying a new wardrobe. I'd like Allegro to buy me white smocks to protect my clothes. I'll wash and press them myself."

The image of Clem delivering supplies to a casino in a starched, white butcher's coat was irresistible. I agreed.

I thought he looked distinctly professional in his new uniform; the warehouse workers thought otherwise. They whistled and hooted, making fun of his white coat when he pulled up to the loading dock. But Clem, who always seemed to march to his own beat, strummed his guitar as he waited for the workers to unload his truck and ignored their teasing. Eventually, they stopped whistling.

Clem had planned to work for me for only a few months, but he ended up staying with me in various roles for more than fifteen years. He was one of the brightest, most multitalented employees I ever hired—and by far the quirkiest.

The goal in the food distribution business is to get in and out of the loading docks as quickly as possible. The less time you expend visiting more docks, the more money you make. Clem was a genius at this. After driving the truck for only a month or two, he figured out that the most efficient way to get in and out of six casinos in an eight-hour shift was to work with the foremen in charge of the individual loading docks. In fact, he may have introduced *slotting* in Atlantic City, which is common practice in the trucking business nowadays but wasn't widely used at the time in the casino industry.

Basically, slotting involves working out a time slot with each foreman to deliver your goods, as opposed to showing up randomly, when other trucks could be lined up ahead of you. By doing this, Clem was generally able to finish work in seven hours.

The loading dock operators took special care of Clem because he helped improve their productivity. And my company's credibility increased because of it.

Clem was brilliant. Clem could also be incredibly difficult. He was definitely not a yes-man and was never shy about offering his opinion on every decision I made, whether it was welcome or not. Usually it wasn't. But Clem had a unique point of view that often gave me a valuable perspective of a situation, although at the time he offered it, it felt like his agenda was to rub my nose in the truth as he saw it.

Most businessmen wouldn't stand for this kind of *insubordination* from employees. On the other hand, successful businesswomen often hire diverse individuals to create a unique mix of personalities among employees, which invigorates a business.[5]

In most traditionally managed businesses, having an employee question the employer's decisions is not tolerated. Women have a different take on running a business. They encourage employees to point out problems and offer suggestions—in effect, get them to *take ownership* in the business—which increases productivity and correspondingly adds to the company's bottom line.

Clem was a nonconformist who liked to play his guitar and compose music in the truck while he waited during pickups and deliveries. My unbiased approach to talented employees led me to see past Clem's idiosyncrasies and recognize his assets. An honest, hardworking guy with a song in his heart, he not only got the job done, but through his innovations he helped establish my company's credibility and contributed significantly to its success.

Clem left New Jersey and my company when he heard California calling him. His parting gift to me was a list of "Do's and Don'ts" that showed me just how much he cared about my meat company (a business I purchased, which will be introduced to you in the next chapter) and what a unique talent he had brought to the company and to me. Here's part of his list, just as he gave it to me.

CLEM'S LIST OF DO'S AND DON'TS

- Have the two sewer lines on the plant side sucked out monthly or the whole neighborhood will stink.

- Make sure Art puts bleach and salt on the back dock every spring to stop the insects from hatching eggs.

- Keep large rodent traps set by the railroad tracks on the North end of the Plant.

- Call exterminator at first sign of bees in side entrance to plant.

- When you assign someone to do a job don't do it yourself.

- When you make a plant rule stick to it.

- Delegate, delegate, delegate or you will regret it!

- Don't try to contact me, I will call you sometime, maybe.

After Clem left, I often reread his list and laughed out loud at his blunt commands and personal reprimands; at the same time, I felt the deep sadness that grabs you when something valuable is lost.

Flour Power

On occasion, Clem wasn't available and I had to make the deliveries myself. This was one of the dirty jobs that were part of the business. Usually, the delivery was a last-minute drop-off of a small gourmet item that weighed no more than ten or fifteen pounds.

One Sunday, the pastry chef at the Tropicana Hotel called me at home in a panic. He needed a thousand pounds of a special kind of flour delivered to the hotel immediately. He'd persuaded the supplier to open his warehouse so Allegro could pick it up and deliver it. Clem was nowhere to be found, which left the job to me.

I was ready, willing, and able, but my car wasn't. A two-seater, it wouldn't have held even half the order . . . and I didn't know how to drive the standard-transmission truck. Working myself into somewhat of a panic, I tried to think of what vehicle I could get my hands on to do the job.

The answer was sitting idly in my garage: a ten-year-old Rolls-Royce that my father had given me as a gift after he sold the Eagles.

Big, black, and shiny, the Rolls was an ostentatious car that never left the garage. Not only was it not my style, it cost $1,000 to fix something every time I drove it. That Sunday, however, it was perfect.

I drove the Rolls to the casino with some trepidation, concerned that the workers might resent me for having the audacity to drive such a fancy car for such a pedestrian purpose.

How wrong I was. I did, indeed, create quite a stir when I pulled up to the loading dock at the Tropicana, but not the kind of stir I'd imagined. The workers bent over laughing as they debated loudly about who would back the car into the loading bay. When word filtered back to the buyers in the purchasing department, they all came out to the dock to see the petite woman in the mammoth Rolls-Royce stuffed with twenty fifty-pound bags of flour. And there was white flour everywhere—covering the dash, the seats, the floor mats, the plush royal blue rug in the trunk, and me.

I know that using a fancy antique car to deliver the order that day is a solution that male business owners would have rejected out of hand—but businesswomen have different priorities.

By taking care of the customer's needs above all else, I was merely practicing what women inherently understand, namely, that *people (not cars) come first*. Margaret Heffernan calls this "customer love" and explains that "this devotion to exceeding customer requirements lies both at the heart of what drives women and makes them so successful."[6]

So, what do you do in a situation like that if you don't have a Rolls? Just what I did—think like a woman and **improvise!**

CHAPTER 6

Buying a Pig in a Poke

After two-and-a-half years in food distribution, I realized that as a distributor I was the middleman between buyers and suppliers, which meant I did not control my own success; those who controlled the products controlled my success. So, unless I wanted to be a middleman forever, I needed to make the products I sold.

John W. Gardner wrote, "We are all faced with a series of great opportunities brilliantly disguised as impossible situations."[1] Mine came in the fall of 1987.

I received a call from a man who owned a meat company in Philadelphia called Allied Steaks. He said he'd heard about my success as a food distributor in Atlantic City and had a meat business for sale that he wanted to show me. When I hung up the phone, I had to pinch myself, thinking, *Could this really be a great opportunity that simply fell into my lap?* A few days later, Burt greeted me at his plant.

A man of about seventy, Burt appeared to be in excellent shape. His nose had obviously been broken, maybe several times (I later learned he'd been an amateur boxer in his early years), and his reddish blond eyebrows attested to the natural red of the few strands of hair he still had on his head. His clothes were dated . . . by at least twenty years. The wide-lapelled jacket of his polyester suit was worn over a shiny, imitation satin shirt, accessorized with a treasure trove of jewelry, including three gold necklaces. I also couldn't help but note several gold rings when he shook my hand in greeting.

"What a great opportunity for your company to be in the meat business!" he said, flashing me a big smile.

This was my introduction to one of the greatest salesmen I'd ever met, and though I never would have guessed it at the time, he turned out to be one of my greatest advisers in business.

The meat plant was three old buildings that had been joined together many years before. The ceilings were so low that in many rooms, if you didn't duck, you'd hit your head on the entrance. Even though the plant was dimly lit, I could see that the cement floors were badly cracked, and it was obvious, even to someone as inexperienced as I, that the plant needed a complete makeover.

Nonetheless, to my surprise, my interest was piqued. At that moment, the idea of a woman diving headfirst into the business of raw meat seemed to me . . . well, like an opportunity brilliantly disguised as an impossible situation!

Now, a businessman checking out that plant as a possible business venture would more than likely have rejected it without even getting out of the car. But businesswomen, who rely on their instinct to get past a visual mess—perhaps because they assume they can fix it—see the substance behind it, if any is there to see.

Over the next few weeks, I did some research on Burt's company. On paper, it never made more than a small profit, but Allied Steaks produced quality meat products and supplied a number of national customers. Something in my gut told me this old-time business might just be the opportunity I was looking for. Women make business decisions by collecting all the *details* first—**being knowledgeable** (BE #7, which is explained in the next chapter)—and then defer to their *gut*.[2]

Based on our first meeting, I was more than a little skeptical about Burt's "great opportunity"; so before I agreed to buy the company, I insisted that Burt set up a dinner with buyers from Allied's two largest customers: Marriott Corporation and K-Mart's in-store restaurants. I needed to see and hear for myself that these customers were for real and had as good a relationship with Burt as he represented to me. This is an example of the active and hands-on role successful businesswomen undertake: they personally meet prospective customers in order to assess the value of a company's business relationships before buying the business.

In this case, Burt turned out to be as good as his word. Dinner with the buyers confirmed his credibility and reassured me that my instinct about Allied Steaks was right. Both customers were longtime fans of Burt and his company and welcomed me sincerely and enthusiastically.

Using the banking relationships I'd made during my time with the Eagles, and armed with the financial statements from Allegro, which showed I could run a profitable company, I was able to borrow $300,000, with the business as collateral, and within a few days of the dinner meeting, I owned Allied Steaks.

Making a Silk Purse from a Sow's Ear

Once Allied was mine, however, I began to wonder if this great opportunity might turn out to be an impossible situation after all. The facilities were old and falling apart; many of the machines didn't work properly or were antiquated; the inventory was spread out all over the plant and impossible to control; and while every other company in the industry had loading docks equipped with pallets and a forklift, Allied had two guys loading cases of product by hand, one by one, from a busy Philadelphia sidewalk.

And, adding insult to injury, pigeons were flying in and out of the plant's windows: a USDA violation that carried a big fine and could result in the plant being shut down.

The office management side of the company wasn't much better—there was none! Nothing was computerized. All the invoices and important documents were either typed or written by hand. And it turned out that Burt's largest customer—the one who praised him and Allied Steaks so highly at our dinner meeting—actually needed his orders computerized. Regardless of their good friendship and solid business relationship, the buyer had told Burt that if Allied didn't get a computerized system up and running within three months, he'd have to pull his business from Allied.

Another nightmare was George. The sales contract stipulated that both Burt (the salesman) and his partner George (the operations guy) would have a twelve-month contract to work for my new company. From my first day as a company owner, I knew George had to go. He was loudmouthed and cursed vociferously at employees and suppliers alike. Businesswomen never tolerate abusive and disrespectful behavior. I was very comfortable telling George, "You're fired," less than a week after buying Allied. After giving him the legal reasons why he was an unfit employee, and following a round of letters back and forth, we settled for two months' pay in lieu of a full year's salary, and George was gone. I was now the operations guy.

As with my tennis dress business, I had a lot to learn. Unlike that earlier business, however, the meat plant came with forty employees . . . all of whom knew I had no experience in meat. And then there was the undeniable fact that women had no credibility in the meat business—especially women who wore high heels to work!

If I was ever going to earn the respect of my employees and my customers, I had to learn the business from top to bottom, and learn it fast.

I asked a lot of questions; Burt was more than happy to answer them. And the more I got to know him, the more I understood that beneath his polyester exterior was the mind of an astute *operator* who made friends with complete strangers in minutes. He knew and was well liked by everyone in the meat business and was a much better resource than the Yellow Pages.

He had a great gift, which I learned to appreciate even though he had used this skill to convince me to buy a broken-down business I knew nothing about!

One important detail I shouldn't fail to mention: Burt loved women . . . all women. Tall, fat, short, skinny—it didn't matter. It wasn't a romantic thing for Burt. He just loved the company of females. He thought women were interesting and he liked being around them. This, as you can imagine, put me in the proverbial driver's seat. Burt was comfortable with me, and when I encouraged him to teach me as much as he could about the business, he obliged, with all the gusto this aging bull could muster.

Ironically, the fact that Allied was such a mess when I bought it turned out to be a blessing in disguise. Because everything was so old, I had to replace most of the equipment, a process that gave me the opportunity both to learn the mechanical details of all the machines in the plant and to interact personally with the employees who operated them. Within a few weeks, I was able to understand the production processes and figure out how to solve most of the problems that cropped up. Spending time on the production floor for hours in the beginning was the best way to learn the operation and get the employees to know me. Businesswomen are different from men in that they genuinely communicate concern for the well-being of their employees, and in return, the employees give their wholehearted commitment to their job.[3]

BE #6 BEING INCLUSIVE (REPRISE)

Because **being inclusive** is such a far-reaching Briefcase Essential that applies to all three of the business categories of "people" that are at the core of any business—your suppliers, your customers, and your employees—I have repeated it in this chapter. When I purchased Allied, I had a whole new set of business dynamics: forty employees. By treating every employee as a unique individual and working directly with each person, I was able to accelerate my understanding of the business and create a positive working atmosphere almost immediately. Never underestimate the strength of leadership that women possess by championing the maxim that **being inclusive** implies that *people come first.*

Within a month, I knew everyone by name—something neither Burt nor his partner had bothered to learn. By knowing their names, asking specific questions about their assigned jobs, and recognizing them as individuals, I was acknowledging that they were important to the business, an attitude that lifted the spirits in the plant overnight. By working directly with line workers and machine operators and asking them for their input, and actually putting many of their suggestions into practice, I had shown them I was a different kind of business owner.

A businesswoman's approach is 180 degrees apart from the way that most men run a business. It is worth repeating that in all my business ventures, I found that communicating with my employees on a personal level encouraged teamwork and fostered a positive attitude that always benefited the bottom line.[4] Margaret Heffernan finds support for her thesis that business materially benefits from "high employee commitment" in *The Enthusiastic Employee: How Companies Profit by Giving Workers What They Want*, which concludes that, "Enthusiastic workers have been shown to increase the quality of their work by a huge percentage—up to a 75 percent reduction in defect rates."[5]

Allied Steaks had everything it needed to be successful: hardworking employees, good customers, and good products. The rest was just problem solving. Although I made some dumb moves and rookie mistakes, the business was fundamentally solid and withstood my inexperience.

I quickly became comfortable in my role as the new owner and was successful, by using every businesswoman's Briefcase Essentials, in growing a male-dominated meat business that had been run into the ground by its former male owners.

CHAPTER 7

The Devil Is in the Details

Businesswomen know the details of their business. Getting the details takes research and information gathering, a process in which women excel because, as we've already seen, women ask for help, ask lots of questions, and cast a wide net among potential sources by personally interacting with others at all levels.

My experience with Allied Steaks taught me just how important it is to get the details about every aspect of the business right from the start. In the meat business, the details start with the raw beef that comes in the door to be processed—something I knew nothing about.

Where's the Beef?

So, it may surprise you to learn that I felt at home with the meat business from the beginning, even though this career move was not a common one for a woman in 1987—and still isn't today. In fact, in the twenty years I owned Allied, I met very few women in either ownership or management roles in the industry. Nonetheless, I found the meat business receptive to businesswomen . . . provided they came armed with knowledge.

One of the first things I learned was that the business was notorious for selling one thing and delivering something else, but I quickly figured out how to provide the watchful eye it required.

My first big challenge as the owner of Allied was a bloody one.

Most days, fresh, raw meat arrived at Allied in thousand-pound cardboard barrels, each of which should have been checked and weighed. Burt and his former partner never checked or weighed the meat Allied received. Checking each barrel would have required visual inspection by removing the top pieces of meat and scrutinizing the meat underneath to confirm that it also was in good condition. Weighing thousand-pound barrels required a scale, a really *big* scale, and really big scales cost really big bucks, so Allied never bought one.

I observed the meat receiving process for a week or two. Every time I watched, it bothered me that we accepted deliveries without checking any of the product. Like most women, when I order something, I examine it carefully to make sure it's what I ordered; if not, I return it. Here I was in a new business, and I found myself disregarding a practice that I had always followed as a consumer, and my common sense was telling me this needed to change.

About two weeks after I bought Allied, I received a shipment of five thousand pounds of raw meat from a large international distributor who had been Allied's supplier for many years. I'd observed the inadequate receiving process long enough and was determined on that day to check out the consistency of the meat and confirm the weights . . . one way or another.

"How do we know that all the meat in the barrel is good without inspecting the meat under the top pieces?" I questioned Burt.

"We've never had a problem, so why should we check it?" he replied.

Questioning him further, I asked, "Why is it that we never spot-check the barrels to make sure we're receiving the weight that's on the invoice?" "I trust the suppliers," he replied. "They're big companies. They wouldn't short-weight us."

"Well, I'm just gonna weigh some meat and see if the weight matches my receiving ticket," I said.

Burt turned to me as if to dare me. "It's impossible, Susan," he said. "We only have small scales. You'll never be able to weigh a whole barrel."

Impossible!? I'd heard that before.

As I headed toward the first thousand-pound barrel, I turned back to Burt and shouted to him, "Watch me."

After washing my hands, I grabbed a large plastic bag, stuck my hands into the barrel, and started pulling out pieces of raw meat and stuffing them into the bag. I weighed the bag on a small scale in the processing room and recorded the weight. I continued this process for another four or five bags before asking two plant employees who had helped me weigh the initial bags to follow my lead and finish the barrel.

When all the meat in the barrel was weighed, we discovered that the barrel content was short by seventy-five pounds. Burt merely rolled his eyes as I instructed the workers to weigh the other four barrels the same way.

It took two hours, but in the end, my suspicion had been confirmed: the weight of each barrel was off, some by as much as a hundred pounds. All together, the barrels held 4,625 pounds of meat, which meant I was paying for 375 pounds of product I never received.

Burt walked over to me and issued an ultimatum of sorts. "Let it go, Susan," he said. "If you take a claim, these guys will never want to sell to you again."

"If I don't take a claim, I'll be out of business in no time," I said.

When Burt finally realized I wasn't going to back down, he took a deep breath and sighed. "Okay . . . okay," he said. "I'll call the supplier to tell the salesman about the short weights and see if I can smooth things over for you."

"That's alright, Burt. I think I'll call, tell our sales rep I'm the new owner, and let him know we have a problem."

"Careful, Susan," Burt cautioned, "it's a huge company and we need them."

"If they charge us for meat we never received, we're better off without them," I said.

With that, I went to my office.

Now, my "office" consisted of a small area divided from the rest of the plant floor by a partial wall. In it was a ten-foot-long wooden plank that served as a desk, and three old chairs with broken wheels that bumped along if you tried to move them. It was an office and desk that I shared with Burt and Mary, who took the orders. But Mary couldn't type, so she spent her days writing out the invoices by hand and then running to the library down the street to make copies. Not exactly the swankiest of operations, but a fancy office was low on my list of priorities. My plan was to limit expenditures to capital improvements that would increase our productivity or generate new business.

In fact, I never did have a real office at the old plant, because unlike men—who seem to have a need to *mark their territory* by immediately redecorating their office—women in business spend money on necessities, not trappings that do not contribute to the bottom line.

She Said, He Said

So, I called the sales rep from my supplier and introduced myself.

"Mike," I said, "I weighed the combos of fresh meat that arrived today at the plant, and found the net weight 375 pounds short."

"That's impossible," he said. "You're new to the business and you don't know what you're doing."

"Mike," I said, "I've been around the block a few times, and where I come from, I only pay for something I receive. I'll be taking a $500 deduction from the invoice to account for the weight discrepancy."

"If you do that without authorization, we'll cut you off and never sell to you again," he said angrily.

"Do what you feel you have to do, but I'm sending your company the weight sheets we recorded on this shipment. As my salesman, you'll need to come to the plant today to verify the weights, even if your company never sells us another piece of meat."

This was true and the salesman knew it. Fresh meat in combos (meaning the meat is "naked," that is, the pieces are not individually encased in plastic) lasts only about four days before the product becomes too contaminated to use. And every day it sits, it loses more and more moisture as the blood drains out, reducing the weight of the meat. Therefore, if a customer makes a claim, in writing, on fresh meat shipped in combos, and the salesperson doesn't show up the same day, there'd be no way for the customer to prove the claim.

"Well, it's already 2:30, and my office is over an hour away from your plant," Mike said, hoping to wiggle out of the trip.

I knew that when Mike verified the short weights, I'd have a chance to connect personally with him, gain credibility, and get a $500 credit for that invoice. I also knew that if he did not show up, I'd be billed in full for the shipment, with little recourse.

"Not a problem, Mike. I'll be happy to wait for you here with donuts and a fresh pot of coffee," I cheerfully responded.

Perhaps he was curious . . . or surprised that I **stood my ground** (BE #8, which is explained in the next chapter) . . . or knew he could potentially have a problem if his boss asked him about the weight sheet sent in by Allied and he had done nothing . . . or any combination of these possibilities. Whatever the reason, Mike said he'd be at the plant by 4:00.

Allied's plant was old and dingy, with cement floors that were always wet and slippery. And, even though it was worlds away from the beautifully appointed offices of the Eagles, I dressed every day in high heels and a tailored suit.

When Mike arrived, he took one look at me and said, "You look like you're in the cosmetics business, not the meat business."

I snickered slightly, grasped his hand, and, giving it a firm shake, looked him in the eyes.

"Mike," I said, "I'm just another meathead. If you decide to work with me, you'll find out how much we have in common."

Mike laughed out loud. Turning to Burt, he said, "How far did you have to chase this gal before convincing her to buy your business?"

Burt smiled. Turning on his charm, he replied: "Mike, you better watch out. Susan is about to give your company a run for its money. She's a stickler for details."

Holding onto a remaining bit of skepticism, Mike checked out the short weights by looking at a few barrels and reviewing the weight sheets I'd recorded. Then he agreed to sign off on the claim.

BE #7 BEING KNOWLEDGEABLE

Women leaders get a leg up in business because they acquire a solid foundation of knowledge about their business.

The more information you accumulate that is relevant to a particular issue, the better the result you will achieve.

By recording in detail the weight of each barrel of meat, not only was I able to obtain credit for the short weight from the salesman; I also had an opportunity to demonstrate that I was a serious professional who backed up action with facts. In other words, I gained credibility.

Being knowledgeable lets others know you know your stuff. It also often distinguishes the business-management technique of women from businessmen, who generally delegate the details to others. As the authors of *How Remarkable Women Lead* so aptly wrote, "Knowledge builds competence, competence builds reputation, and reputation opens doors."[1]

"I gotta tell you, Susan, I'm impressed," Burt said to me once Mike had left.

In a joking way, I replied, "Burt, if you'd weighed your meat over the past thirty years, you'd be a millionaire by now, and I'd never have been able to afford to buy your company!"

Burt smiled and shook his head. He couldn't help but agree with what I said, but he seemed to appreciate my attempt to make light of it rather than to imply that he and his partner were foolish businessmen. I knew that, despite his easy-going manner, Burt was very sensitive.

Women pay special attention to the feelings of others because they want to foster good relationships, whether it's in business or life. Understand that pointing out a man's mistakes never gets you ahead; it only creates animosity and resentment.

By the way, Mike continued to sell me fresh meat for another fifteen years. With the $500 I saved on my initial claim, I bought a large pre-owned scale, which allowed me to weigh a whole barrel at a time. And, with Burt as my constant source of both moral support and facts about the meat business, Allied Steaks continued to grow and prosper.

CHAPTER 8

La Femme Phobique

In the last chapter, I described my experience with the meat salesman who gave me a hard time before agreeing to visit my Allied Steaks plant to verify my short weights. He's an example of a *hard-core* male working in a *hard-core* male business—that is, a man working in a male-dominated business who has had little, if any, experience working with women business owners.

However, he is not what I call a *female-phobic* male—that is, a man who will not recognize women as qualified business-persons and therefore refuses to do business with them directly. They may not be consciously aware of why they do what they do, but such men put these women down, ignore them, or otherwise marginalize them—in blatant or subtle ways—thus limiting their business opportunities. Women need to identify female-phobic men and find a way around them . . . because they will never change!

Let me tell you about my experience with *La Femme Phobique*.

When I was starting Allegro Foods, my food distribution business, I was determined to learn as much as possible about the products I was about to handle, especially because I never cooked anything but microwave popcorn! I read books, spoke with a well-known food critic I knew, and made dinner out every night a part of my education. I picked apart dishes as if I were an analytical scientist, trying to identify the type of meat and ingredients that were used to create them.

I was a good student and studied all the relevant details; in a short time, I knew my own products inside out. For any cut of meat I sold, I knew the animal's genetics, its characteristics, and the way the cut was created. I could trace the origins of a calf and tell you what it was fed, how it was raised, and how it compared to similar products. Most other distributors didn't even know what end of the animal they were selling.

Once I felt confident in my ability to talk *gourmet*, I met with many casino chefs to tell them about my products, in particular the meat products. Most of the chefs had never dealt with a distributor who was a woman, let alone one who sold meat products, but once they sampled the natural veal cutlets and prime steaks I brought, they treated me the same way they would any other meat distributor. One chef, however, wouldn't give me the time of day: François was a man who had studied with some of the most famous chefs in Paris.

The first time I went to see François, he turned his back on me, barked orders to his two *sous*-chefs, and even took a personal phone call while I was in his office.

None of the other chefs I'd met with had ever given me anything but their undivided attention. So, it was clear to me that François was a hard-core male who had an incurable anti-woman bias and that he had already made up his mind before our meeting a woman could not offer him anything of interest. After giving it my best shot and getting nothing but disrespectful treatment in return, I politely said my "thank-yous" to François and the *sous*-chefs, who nodded sheepishly as I left.

I was determined to sell to François. His restaurants were the largest users of fresh, natural veal in Atlantic City, and I knew I had a product that was not only of better quality but also substantially less expensive. I just had to figure out how to get around his all too apparent bias against businesswomen. I opened my briefcase and took out my talents of **being persistent** (BE #2) and **being improvisational** (BE #4).

In the course of getting my food distribution business up and running, I'd met and befriended a young liquor salesman. Frankie was handsome, suave, always well dressed, relatively articulate . . . and male—exactly the kind of person I thought François would listen to.

I told Frankie of my situation and asked if he'd be willing to help me out. I let him know up front that if he'd meet with François and me, and was able to get the chef to buy my veal, I'd arrange for him and a guest to dine at the Sands Casino (one of my best customers) at the gourmet restaurant of his choice. *Quid pro quo!*

Now, Frankie knew nothing about veal other than what I explained to him thirty minutes before the meeting, but François listened to Frankie as if he were a professor. As for me, I stood in the background and said nothing. In no time, Frankie convinced François to sample the veal. By the end of the meeting, I had the business.

When dealing with female-phobic men, be creative and take advantage of your Briefcase Essentials, as I did, to *beat them at their own game.*

Bullies

As almost any woman can tell you, there are bound to be times—in both life and business—when a man's behavior is not a case of bias against women in business; it is bullying, plain and simple. Male bullies try to dominate and intimidate a woman physically, verbally, or both. It's important for women to recognize that in these circumstances, they do have certain advantages, and they don't have to be intimidated.

Business negotiations are often, if not always, about power. The following incidents were confrontational and stressful, but they are nevertheless illustrative of how a woman who uses her Briefcase Essentials can take control of a difficult situation with a run-of-the-mill bully.

Three Blind Mice

In 1989, I bought a ham processing company. That's a whole story in itself, which I'll get to in the next chapter, but for now, all you need to know is that soon after buying the ham company,

I ran into an ugly situation with the macho buyer for my single biggest customer—which happened to be one of the largest purchasers of deli meats in the Northeast region of the country.

I was in danger of losing the contract. Mickey, a paunchy, forty-five-year-old man who wore a bad hairpiece and a signature bit of jewelry—three silly-looking silver mice pinned to the collar of his shirt—turned out to be not only obnoxious but also physically aggressive.

Halfway into our first meeting—a dinner he had arranged—Mickey dismissed his sales manager, leaving himself alone with me. As soon as the sales manager was gone, Mickey moved closer to me. I tried to move away without being obvious, but it didn't work. When he tried to put his hands on my leg under the table, I got up to go to the ladies' room. When I returned, it happened again. I excused myself a second time, realizing that if it happened a third time and I rebuffed him, it would be awkward and embarrassing for him, and I'd probably lose the business.

Fortunately, by the time I got back to the table the second time, Mickey was drunk, and I had several men escort him out to his car (in those days, no one called for a taxi). I had survived *round one* with the buyer, but business issues remained to be solved, and I knew that before we met again, I had to have a plan.

I decided to get all the dirt on Mickey I could from someone who knew him well, to see if I could learn anything that might give me an advantage to win *round two*.

Robbie, my sales manager, knew Mickey ... and was not a fan. So I called Robbie into my office on the day after my first meeting with the buyer and asked a couple of leading questions, to which he gave me more than an earful; he seemed to enjoy spilling the beans.

"Mickey's got the worst reputation in the business!" Robbie said.

It seems that Mickey had been with the same company for almost twenty years, during which he had gained a lot of power. So, despite his notorious reputation for intimidating women and putting them into compromising situations, apparently, his superiors were either unaware of Mickey's obnoxious behavior or chose not to call him on the carpet because he continued this sexist conduct with impunity.

In fact, *obnoxious* is too kind a description for Mickey's actions. I was both shocked and relieved to learn that I'd somehow escaped the way Mickey usually greeted a woman—*any* woman—which was to put his tongue in her mouth.

Robbie also told me something I already knew—Mickey drank a lot, and he routinely was drunk before the meal was over.

When I asked Robbie if he could give me any advice on how to handle Mickey, he simply said, "Stay away."

Pressing him for more information, I asked if he thought we could do our business in the office and then send Mickey on his way.

"No chance," said Robbie, shaking his head. "He only conducts business out of the office. It's usually a dinner meeting . . . and he never pays."

After speaking with Robbie, I realized that if I was going to win over this buyer—keeping both the business *and* my dignity—I needed to bring someone along with me to the next meeting who understood the problem and could watch my back. The only executive man in my organization at the time was Robbie. Unfortunately, he was spineless, and I knew I couldn't count on him to come to my aid.

I did, however, have a very savvy CFO. Barbara was a slim, attractive blonde in her late thirties and my right-hand "man." I told her about Mickey's inappropriate amorous advances.

She agreed to come with me to the next dinner meeting, and we devised a plan.

The meeting took place at Lamberti's, a local, upscale Italian restaurant. When we arrived, Mickey lit up at the sight of Barbara. He didn't know she was coming, but he was only too happy to be dining with not one, but two attractive women.

I introduced her to Mickey as a consultant to Allied, and Barbara extended her hand. Sure enough, Mickey moved in to kiss her. Forewarned, Barbara turned her head as if to look around the restaurant, and his lips only grazed her cheek.

When we got to the table, we sat on either side of Mickey, understanding that he'd have to turn his head constantly to talk to each of us, leaving him little time or concentration to play tricks under the table. When he got up to go to the rest room, we took the opportunity to do the same—together—so we were never separated from each other.

Mickey was so happy to have two educated women at his table (blondes, no less!), both of whom were giving him lots of attention, asking him questions about his favorite subject—himself—that instead of making unwanted advances, he just laughed, made jokes, and relaxed. He basked in the envious looks and comments from other men walking by, and he was so busy holding court and trying to amuse us that he forgot about trying to grab a leg under the table.

Seeing him so happy and at ease, I got up the nerve to ask him why he wore the three mice. His answer was as silly as the silver mice themselves: he had always wanted to serve in the army and wear ribbons and silver ornaments on his collar, but because he never was given the chance, he wore the mice in place of stars.

Mickey laughed as if this was the funniest thing in the world, and we laughed right along with him.

"Some hero," I said to Barbara as we left the restaurant.

We laughed again, both at the repugnant man we'd just had dinner with and because our *two gals are better than one* plan, intended to keep Mickey distracted, had worked.

I ended up keeping the contract and preserving the relationship with Mickey, although I made sure I never had to go out with him again: about a month after the dinner, I hired a salesman, Richard, who did the *guy thing* with Mickey.

Bullies are a difficult challenge, but practicing safety in numbers works every time.

Men in Blue

Power comes in many forms; sometimes, it's embodied in a badge.

In the early spring of 2004, I was in my office, across the street from my Allied Steaks plant in Vineland, New Jersey, when I got a frantic call from the manager of the plant. Two men he'd never seen before had entered the plant, flashing badges. I hung up and ran to the plant.

Once inside, I saw two men taking pictures of a large meat tumbler located in the middle of the raw grinding room. I immediately approached them and told them to leave. Although they identified themselves as Occupational Safety and Health Administration (OSHA) inspectors, with the right to inspect any plant, any time, without notice, I was not daunted.

"You have no right to be in a federally inspected meat plant without following the rules of the plant," I said, and then recited my rules to them.

"Everyone who enters this plant is required to wash their hands and dip their shoes in a sanitized bath. And they must wear a hair net, a hard hat, and a clean white factory coverall," I said. "Furthermore, you have no right to take pictures of my proprietary equipment."

The pleasant-looking, younger inspector—he was about thirty-five—was more reasonable than his superior, a fiftyish, red-faced man who was belligerent and ready for a fight.

Walking the younger inspector toward the exit, I said, "Let's go over to my office and discuss this."

He was ready to follow me out of the plant, but the lead inspector refused to go. Instead, he moved to the entrance of one of the cook rooms, took out some kind of meter, and began to record numbers.

"What are you doing?" I asked.

The lead inspector said nothing.

I managed to usher the inspectors into the plant office, adjacent to the cook room, where three male supervisors were working. They paid us no mind as I repeated the company regulations to the inspectors and suggested they come over to my office where we could establish the ground rules.

The lead inspector merely scoffed at this request. It was apparent this bully was not used to being challenged, and he was exhibiting an obvious bias toward me because I was a woman.

"What regional office are you from, and who's in charge there?" I asked.

"South Jersey; but I don't have to tell you the name of my boss," he replied with a sneer.

Supported by my very limited knowledge of agency law, which I had learned in law school, I demanded to see the regulations and authority that allowed them to storm into my plant without following plant sanitary regulations and to continue taking pictures after I'd asked them to stop.

The lead inspector looked at me like I was crazy. "I have an OSHA badge," he said, as if a badge gave him inalienable rights to do whatever he wanted.

"I don't care," I said. "Your badge is useless without the regulations that show you're authorized to enter this plant."

I noticed that the supervisors had stopped working and stood with their mouths agape watching the standoff. Then I saw the young inspector start to walk toward the exit. The lead inspector hesitated a moment, but he also turned toward the exit.

At this point, I knew I had him.

I followed the inspectors outside to their car.

"Before you leave, I'd like to see a copy of your regulations," I asked again.

Neither responded, which indicated to me they didn't have the necessary papers with them.

"Maybe we should go to her office with her," the younger man said to the elder.

"No. I'll be back, and she'll be sorry," he threatened, showing both anger and surprise that I had refused to back down and, at least for now, had gotten the better of them.

I walked over to the passenger side of the car where the younger man was about to get in and calmly asked: "Can you give me the name and telephone number of your boss? And by the way, what were you measuring in the cook room with your meter?"

Almost in a whisper, so the lead inspector wouldn't hear, he said, "Noise."

Then he got in the car and they drove away.

After they left, I went back to my office and immediately called the South Jersey office of OSHA and spoke to the head of the department, who was pleasant and cordial. Business-women go right to the source and rely on their communication skills to start a congenial discussion with the person in charge.

When I identified myself and described what had just happened, he apologized for his inspectors, agreeing that they should have complied with the sanitary regulations of the plant.

"Were they allowed to take pictures in my plant?" I asked, already sure of his answer.

"Not without permission from the owner," he replied.

"And the meter . . . what was that for?"

"It's a portable noise meter that measures decibel levels in a given area," he explained. "Based on the information reported to me by the inspectors who just left your plant, you might have a problem."

"It's interesting that your inspector called you from his car instead of waiting until he returned to your office to make his report," I said. "And, I have to tell you that he didn't leave without delivering a veiled threat to me. I consider his bullying manner out of line."

The supervisor apologized again. "I don't want any trouble, ma'am," he said. "I'm going to send a new team out in a few months, and I'll be sure to let you know before they come."

I quickly realized that **standing up** to the inspector's bullying and overt bias gave me a distinct advantage. The fact that a woman questioned his authority gave him pause as well as put his boss in a defensive position. He now had to take special care to ensure that his inspectors treated me fairly and gave me the same consideration they'd give to a male plant owner.

This bought me some wiggle room not usually enjoyed by male owners: time to gain the knowledge necessary to address the OSHA issues so we'd be prepared for the next inspection.

BE #8   BEING ABLE TO STAND YOUR GROUND

One of the most attention-grabbing things a woman can do is to act in a way that takes a businessman by surprise. Men have a tendency to underestimate a woman's grit in business and often are caught flat-footed because they are unprepared when a businesswoman is **able to stand her**

ground. Offering an unflinching and valid argument based in fact is the best way to disarm a bully. It's what I call an effective "biased bully repellent." Taking this action (at the right time and place) will elevate your credibility a thousandfold and lift your spirits.

Because the lead OSHA inspector, a biased man with a badge, never expected me to stand up to his bullying, I gained a valuable advantage when I continued to maintain my position.

Several months later, we had our official OSHA inspection. The agency confirmed that we needed to enforce the earplug rule, which thanks to the consultant we'd had time to hire, was already in place. As a result, the company saved a significant amount of money on fines we most likely would have received, and like any successful businesswoman, I used this situation to my advantage by beginning and maintaining a dialogue with an important official at OSHA—just in case I needed help in the future.

CHAPTER 9

There's No Crying in Business . . . or Is There?

Crying in a business situation is generally viewed as a sign of a woman's weakness, but there are exceptions to this precept. I recall two instances of crying in a business setting that illustrate the significant impact crying can have on observers—for better or for worse.

Crybaby

Two years after I bought Allied Steaks, my old friend and adviser, Burt, brought me another *great opportunity*. His son-in-law's family owned a $50-million ham processing company that was facing a forced sale: the USDA was threatening to close it down for improper business practices unless it was sold to a legitimate buyer.

By now, I knew Burt (the operator) had more than just my interests in mind. As always, there was the *quid pro quo*; in this case, it was a $50,000 finder's fee that the sellers promised him if I bought the company.

Unlike Allied, the ham company looked good on paper. Although it wasn't making much money, it had good customers and produced a broad range of deli products in an impressive facility with state-of-the-art equipment. It looked like I could come in, run the business lean and mean, and make a significant profit.

Perhaps it was my ego telling me I could turn anything around at this point in my career, or perhaps it was simply negligence, but the fact was that I ignored my talent of **being knowledgeable** (BE #7) and didn't do my homework, my due diligence. The company looked so good, I didn't question the validity of the information I was given or the veracity of those giving it.

I should have kept in mind that even when you do everything right, someone else could do something dishonest. In this case, I was sucker punched about the quality of the products and the true state of the company's relationship with its customers. Ironically, while Allied's success reaffirmed my belief that a company's employees, products, and customers are the three assets a business needs to be successful, I ended up buying a company that had only one out of three—employees!

Rather than cry over spilled milk, I did what any businesswoman would do—I rolled up my sleeves, learned all the details of the ham company, and then made it my own. I renamed it Suzannah Farms.

However, in 1991, after three years of incredibly long hours and hard work, I had nothing to show for my efforts except significant losses. It was time to face the cold reality that unless something changed drastically, I'd need to find a buyer for the company as quickly as possible. In the meantime, I had to keep the company afloat.

Make no mistake about it; this is a painful and anguish-filled process that will test your ability to lead and one that requires every ounce of inner strength you can muster.

Barbara, my CFO, who you met in chapter 8 as my "partner in crime" to accompany me at dinner with Mickey the bully, was a CPA, with extensive training as an accountant and a great deal of experience working for major national companies. Although she had no experience operating a private company, let alone a financially troubled private company, she seemed eager to accept the challenge I offered her.

Most days, she sat in my office with me trying to figure out how to meet our expenses. That old bugaboo cash flow—having enough income from sales coming in to cover the money going out for expenses—returned once again. This time it was the almost half-million dollars a week I needed to cover payroll and expenses, and more often than not I was short . . . a reality that put Barbara constantly in a state of panic.

One day, just after Barbara had run payroll and discovered that there was not enough money to cover the checks that were already printed, she rushed into my office, fell into a chair, and started crying hysterically. The tears streaming down her face dragged streaks of black mascara with them.

Unfortunately, this was in plain view of anyone who happened to look through the large glass windows of my office—a potentially disastrous situation. If the employees saw the CFO crying in my office, they'd know the company was in trouble and would be out looking for new jobs . . . and the company would die a quick, certain death.

To be clear, in a situation such as this, an inability to control one's emotions at work, in plain view of others, is a huge *disadvantage* that can destroy your credibility.

My initial reaction to the sight of this very competent woman reduced to a soggy mass of tears was one of frustration and distaste. I wanted to shake her and tell her to get a hold of herself—anything to stop the flood—but I could see she was already overwhelmed. So, I looked her in the eye and calmly told her I understood why she was upset, but that I wanted her to stop crying and to go to the ladies' room and fix her makeup. I promised her that by the time she returned to the office, I'd have worked out a plan to cover the cash shortfall.

A businessman would have written her off as weak and unreliable, but women in business are problem solvers—who reach different conclusions—because they do not rely on gender stereotyping to make personnel evaluations. Instead, we consider the total person.

Appealing to Barbara's rational side did the trick. She stopped crying, left the office, and within ten minutes, was back, dry-eyed and freshly made up. I kept my word and explained to her, in detail, how we were going to fix the problem by using an indispensable Briefcase Essential—**being resourceful.**

BE #9 BEING RESOURCEFUL

Being resourceful, one of the most important skills in any business and an invaluable talent that businesswomen need to work on, is the ability to think imaginatively—in a new and original way—to solve serious problems. Solving the problems of an ailing company on its last legs requires bold initiatives and an ingenious action plan in order to achieve success; and, even then, there are no guarantees. The good news is, this is something that women handle better than men. Helen Fisher explains it this way: "As women make decisions, they weigh more variables, consider more options and outcomes, recall more points of view, and see more ways to proceed."[1]

My solution was to stretch payment to my suppliers past their seven-day terms one day at a time until we were actually paying them in fourteen or twenty-one days. I knew that they knew that if they demanded payment in full immediately, and we could not pay it, they'd eventually force us into bankruptcy, which would end their chance of getting paid in full. Their only other option would be to accept our offer and extend our terms ... unofficially. This was a new concept for Barbara, who had only worked for large corporations and therefore was never taught how to deal with cash-flow problems. Once I described the plan in detail, she was able to go with the flow—so to speak.

CFOs who work solely for Fortune 500 companies rarely (if ever) have to deal with issues of cash flow; consequently, they never need to learn and certainly never show others how to manage a cash shortfall. But it's something *all* small business owners know about firsthand.

Barbara learned from this experience, practiced the Briefcase Essentials, and continued to work as my company accountant for fifteen years ... without shedding another tear. We remain close friends and professional associates to this day.

Cry, Baby

We did manage to keep Suzannah Farms from tanking as I tried to find a local buyer for the company. After almost a year of focused practice of **being persistent** (BE #2), yet searching in vain, I turned to a large ham company in Detroit. In fact, it was one of the companies whose payables we'd stretched—*really* stretched—in order to pay our employees. My company was currently on the hook to Mid-West Pork for about $800,000, and therefore I had real leverage. When I called the company's comptroller to tell him I wanted to pay him a visit in Detroit, he jumped at the suggestion, because he thought I wanted to work out a deal to pay off our debt. What I really wanted to do was have a personal meeting with the chairman of Mid-West Pork and pitch him on the virtues of buying my company.

When I arrived at Mid-West Pork's headquarters, I found the company to be much larger than I expected. Although the Detroit plant was its flagship, Mid-West Pork had several plants in other western cities. The chairman of the board's father had started the company fifty years earlier and, since then, it had made many additions. By the time I visited, it took up a large city block.

I was given a quick tour of the slaughter facilities and processing areas and was then escorted to the executive offices, where I was led down a long corridor to the comptroller's office. Most comptrollers I did business with as creditors were a cheerless breed, especially when I owed them as much money as my company owed Mid-West Pork. Joe, on the other hand, was a pleasant man in his mid-thirties, and he seemed genuinely happy to meet me. He rose from behind his desk and greeted me warmly. I could tell from his facial expression and body language that he was approachable and surprisingly unguarded.

"How long have you been with Mid-West Pork?" I asked after the usual pleasantries.

"The chairman and I were college buddies and he brought me into the business about ten years ago," he said, settling me into a comfortable chair.

Walking back to his seat behind his desk, Joe wasted no time asking me the $800,000 question—"How do you intend to pay off the money you owe us?"—but before I could answer, he made a surprising admission. "It's my fault we let your company build up such a huge payable," he said.

Attempting to lessen the weight of his somber confession, I said, "Well, when an opportunity presents itself, I just try to take advantage of it, like any good businessperson."

My response seemed to take him by surprise, and he let out a hearty laugh, dissipating the tension in the air.

"Susan, are you here because your company is in trouble and you want to try to work things out?" he asked.

"Yes and no," I replied.

He seemed momentarily at a loss for words, but then made another confession. "Well, I can tell you this," he said, "no company owing us as much as your company owes us right now—and could stick us for the money—has ever asked to come see us face-to-face."

I smiled cordially and said, "Well, Joe, I'm here to offer you a great opportunity." I watched the look on his face turn to surprise, then to curiosity as I continued. "My company would be a perfect fit with Mid-West Pork."

I knew that the only way I could solve my company's dire state of affairs was by aggressively being **resourceful** and coming up with a bold challenge.

Before he could respond, I confided in him just as he had with me, telling him that if my company couldn't find a buyer, I didn't know how long Suzannah Farms would survive. I also admitted that this was the purpose of my trip.

He told me he appreciated my candor and asked that I fill him in on the business details. When I finished, he stood up. By this time, I was convinced he was an open-minded businessman who would be an advocate for my company's proposal.

"Okay, Susan," he said, "let's go see the chairman."

The chairman, Mr. Dodd, was a short, stern-looking man who had none of the warmth of the comptroller. He greeted me rather coolly and asked why I wanted to sell my company. I started to answer, when Joe interrupted.

"Susan's company produces Krakus hams in her plant, and that would fit nicely with our product line," he said.

Without hesitation, the chairman asked, "If we purchase your company, can you bring the contract to produce Krakus hams to Detroit?"

"I think so," I responded, trying not to show the elation I was feeling with the hope of a sale possibly becoming a reality. "But," I added, "I'll need to go to Poland to get permission."

Mr. Dodd, a testy, old-fashioned businessman, turned to Joe. "Work out the details and get back to me if the numbers work," he said.

Just like that, a deal was in the offing.

A few weeks later, once Mid-West Pork had done its due diligence, the deal was done. The only caveat was that I had to convince my Polish partner to let me sell my company and to agree to transfer the production of the Krakus hams to the Detroit plant. (But that's a whole other story for the next chapter!)

Agreeing to sell to Mid-West Pork meant closing down my company and leaving my employees without their jobs.

According to federal law (the Warn Statute), companies with fifty or more employees were required to give all employees sixty days' notice before shutting down and closing their doors. Rather than issuing a memo or something just as impersonal, which is a standard practice of most male business owners, I met with my workers personally to give them the bad news that, unfortunately, they'd soon be out of work.

It wasn't easy to terminate the people who'd worked so hard for me and, in the same breath, ask them to keep working for another sixty days so I could fulfill my obligation to the new buyer to continue making product. The natural tendency of employees in a situation like this would be, at the very least, to throw in the towel and not work very hard if, in fact, they showed up for work at all. An equally common reaction would be to get angry with the owner and possibly even try to harm the plant or its products in some way before the closing.

By standing up in front of my two hundred employees and explaining to them, one shift at a time, why the business had to move to the only place I could find a buyer, and giving them a brief recap of the efforts I had made to try to save the business, I hoped to let them know that I cared about them, that I'd done my best for them, but that, unfortunately, I couldn't save their jobs . . . and that I was very truly sorry. My actions that day mirror the beliefs held by most women business owners: employees are part of your family and it is your responsibility to protect them. Margaret Heffernan, in *How She Does It*, describes her findings this way: "Every woman-owned business I've ever studied or visited has sooner or later been described to me as a family."[2]

My plan was to tell the story in a calm, clear, unemotional way. But when I stood in front of the workers and looked into the eyes of the men and women I talked to and worked with every day, tears filled my eyes. I couldn't help it, and the tears continued to fall until my speech was finished. I couldn't believe that I had been unable to hide my emotions, and I feared an angry crowd of disappointed workers would mock me. But, as I dried my eyes and tried to regain some composure, one of the workers shouted out, "You're not so tough!" and the rest of the workers applauded and laughed warmly in appreciation.

It was a telling moment for me. As a leader, I knew not to have a buddy-buddy relationship with my employees. I felt it would compromise my ability to be objective and manage effectively. I followed this principle throughout my career; in most cases, it served me well. However, there are times when compassion and **empathy** take over and expose the truth—that you are human. It's a rare moment when most bosses or figures of authority show this side of themselves, but if it's sincere, it's a moment that will be appreciated forever by everyone who witnesses it. Simon Baron-Cohen studied the topic of *empathizing* for five years before his findings were published in *The Essential Difference*,[3] in which he concludes that women are better *empathizers* than are men.[4]

BE #10 BEING EMPATHETIC

Being empathetic is the ability to identify with and understand someone else's feelings or difficulties. Simon Baron-Cohen describes empathy as "a defining feature of human relationships."[5] Empathy comes naturally to most women and is a trait that is an invaluable business tool because it lets

> you look at another person's view of a situation. However, if
> you allow your empathy to cause you to lose control of your
> emotions publicly, nine times out of ten it will backfire on
> you and make you appear weak.

When my tears revealed my true feelings for my employees, they understood I was crying not because I couldn't handle the situation (as was the case with Barbara's outburst), but because I understood the human consequences of my decision: it wasn't just a business that was closing; people's lives were involved. When a plant shuts down, it's traumatic for everyone involved. Shutting down the ham company and closing the plant was an exceptional event that required qualities that most women possess—understanding, kindness, and **empathy**.

Because I communicated openly and honestly with all the employees, every worker stayed on and saw the company through until closing day, saving me from even greater losses. Standing there with a heavy heart, saying *thank you* and *goodbye* to my employees that final day, when the plant closed, I took a silent vow that I'd never shut down another plant. Fourteen years later, I kept my promise.

CHAPTER 10

Another Great Opportunity

In this chapter, you'll learn that many types of communication exist, and that a woman's way of communicating in any language—verbal or not—is one of her most dynamic Briefcase Essentials. Women are natural **communicators**. Men listen . . . women talk . . . to everyone.

Women's ability to communicate is not just about their ability to talk; they also are aware of what others are thinking. Helen Fisher explains it this way: "They pick up the tiny signals that people send, detect their motives and desires—and deftly navigate their way into the human heart."[1] She goes on to attribute this gift to women's senses, all of them (touch, smell, taste, vision, and hearing), which she describes as, "more finely tuned than those of men."[2] These traits, along with other observations that women instinctively notice, such as body language, facial expressions, tone of voice, and body movements, collectively represent what women in business uniquely possess—**the ability to be perceptive communicators.**

BE #11 BEING A PERCEPTIVE COMMUNICATOR

Being a perceptive communicator—one of the Briefcase Essentials I use hundreds of times every day—has been described in every chapter of this book, but I chose to highlight it in chapter 10 to point out the unique way in which **this ability, this talent** can be used to exchange ideas and build relationships.

One day in 1991, I got a call at my Suzannah Farms office from Thomas Gardner, an owner of AKK, the American distributor of internationally recognized Krakus hams. He introduced himself and asked if he and his brother could come to my plant. They had a business proposition for me.

Although still a little gun-shy at the thought of getting involved with yet another *great opportunity*, I was aware of AKK's good reputation as an importer of quality ham products, and I didn't dismiss the possibility that such a company could be of help to Suzannah Farms.

"I'd be happy to give you a personal tour of my plant, Thomas," I said.

He quickly responded, "Is this Friday good for you?"

Now, Krakus hams were, and still are today, regarded as a very high-quality cooked ham product. For almost a century, they were manufactured exclusively in Poland by a government-owned Polish ham company. But it seemed that now the owners of Krakus hams were being forced to diversify the manufacturing of their products by expanding to the United States.

However, the Polish company's American distributor, AKK, based in Elizabeth, New Jersey, didn't have the equipment necessary to make the hams themselves. They needed to find an American partner who could manufacture the hams for them, one that was geographically close, had a state-of-the-art plant, and lots of capacity (unused production time).

Thomas had called me because Suzannah Farms met all of the requirements. He knew this because he'd done some business with my company's former owners.

Thomas and his brother arrived at ten o'clock Friday morning. Tall, skinny, straightforward, and a little stern looking, Thomas was nonetheless enthusiastic. We donned the proper uniforms for the tour—hair net, hard hat, and smock—and washed our hands, then I showed them around every production area . . . all one hundred thousand square feet of it.

Walking into the main cook room during our tour, Thomas turned to me and said, "Your plant is in excellent condition, but it's obviously being underutilized." He then confided, "I want you to know, I'd never have called the former owners with this, Susan."

He explained that he wasn't comfortable with the former owners' business practices, but he'd checked out my background and credentials and was satisfied.

After the tour, Thomas told me of the situation facing the Polish company that resulted in the opportunity for AKK to produce Krakus hams in the United States . . . if he could find an appropriate plant. "A plant like Suzannah Farms," he said.

I was extremely pleased . . . and interested. Not only did this seem to be a real opportunity; I desperately needed the business.

One nonnegotiable condition was that a ham maker of the Polish company's choosing would be 100 percent in charge of the Krakus production. Most ham producers (and, at the time, they were all men) would have balked at that condition. Women in business are more **adaptable** (BE #3), and my company needed the business.

We quickly worked out the terms of our deal, and within a month, Thomas delivered the agreed-upon Polish ham–*meister* to my plant and into my care.

And that's how Suzannah Farms became the first company in America to produce the famous Krakus hams.

Speaking Polish from the Heart

Paul Debrenko, the Polish ham–*meister*, greeted me for the first time with a big, wide smile, firmly took my hand, looked me squarely in the eye, and said something in Polish that I didn't understand.

A short, muscular man with a pleasant face covered partially by a bushy brown mustache that turned up at the ends, Paul had been the manager of a huge Krakus ham plant in Poland for many years. He'd never traveled outside of Europe, and the lines on his face suggested that life had been very difficult in his homeland.

I smiled, greeted him warmly, and told him how happy I was to have him show us the Polish way to make hams. It was obvious that he didn't understand my English any more than I understood his Polish, but I hooked my arm through his, got him outfitted for the tour, and escorted him into the plant.

As I led Paul through each of the processing rooms, he was very animated, gesturing often with his hands as he spoke excitedly in Polish. He was clearly delighted to be in America and in my plant. I could tell, too, that he was completely at ease with me and understood that I'd be his point of contact and interpreter. Most male business owners would have delegated this job to the plant manager. But women in business intuitively understand the importance of building a personal relationship with a new colleague and initiate the process right off the bat.

The Krakus project was a huge piece of new business for Suzannah Farms, and I was aware that its success rested solely on Paul's ability to make it happen the Polish way. As our learning to communicate with each other was critical, I stuck to him like glue. At first, we communicated mostly by hand gestures and body language. Within a month, we understood each other fairly well.

My business skills were pushed to the max during Paul's first month in America. I helped him set up his small apartment a few blocks from the plant, and I checked out the neighborhood for stores within walking distance where he could pick up necessities. Yes, this *is* part of business from a woman's point of view, because women are able to put themselves in another person's shoes, and by **being empathetic**, they do what it takes to help an important associate adapt to a different environment. Without knowing it, I was instinctively building a relationship that social scientists describe as creating "social capital; the relationships between people and the feelings of mutual obligation and support these relationships create."[3]

Paul was generally a mild-mannered manager . . . except when he was unable to communicate what he wanted employees to do. And as many of the employees did not understand him as well as I did, it was not uncommon to see Paul running out of the plant cursing in Polish and demanding to talk to me. But this same intensity, along with Paul's incredible work ethic, which was obvious to the employees at Suzannah Farms, seemed to inject new life into this failing business.

To communicate my appreciation, a few weeks after Paul settled in, I planned a surprise for him. Finding Paul in the plant, I asked him to follow me outside, to my car. Opening the passenger door, I gestured for him to get in. He turned to me and shrugged his shoulders as if to ask, *What's this about?* I smiled and, speaking in a calm, reassuring voice, said, in English: "Relax. We're taking a little excursion."

After driving about thirty minutes, I pulled into a small strip center. Before I even parked, Paul started bouncing up and down in his seat and clapping and laughing at the sight of a large sign written in Polish.

Once the car was parked, he jumped out, ran over to me, gave me a big hug, and asked, "We go now?"

We spent about half an hour in the Polish market, and Paul left with several bags of Polish specialties.

During the entire ride back to the plant, Paul said over and over, "Thank you, thank you!"

I just smiled and said to him, in part English and part Polish, "We go back every two weeks, okay?"

"Okay!" he replied.

Being a perceptive communicator is a powerful tool, especially when building a relationship with a colleague, working with a potential customer, or trying to persuade a business partner to see your point of view. And it's important to understand that words are not the only way to communicate. The Polish ham–*meister* did not speak a word of English when we first met, which meant that I needed to use physical and symbolic communication to connect with him. I made certain that my body language and actions indicated that he was a welcome visitor who was making a valuable contribution to the business.

By the time I took Paul to a Polish market, we could each say a few words in the other's language, but nothing communicated my appreciation more clearly than our semimonthly visits to that store. In this case, deeds were much better than words. Building a real relationship with a stranger takes time, patience, sincerity, and honesty—typical qualities that women share—which explains why businesswomen intuitively practice **perceptive communication**.

About four months after Paul arrived, his Polish boss showed up and found the systems running smoothly . . . and deemed the sample Krakus product acceptable for rollout.

A few weeks later, the hams were introduced successfully into the marketplace, and no one noted any difference between the hams made in Cherry Hill, New Jersey, and those made in Warsaw, Poland.

When in Rome . . . (Okay, When in Poland . . .)

Producing Krakus hams in my plant helped improve the cash flow of my company, but unfortunately, the sales volume was insufficient to put the company in the black.

So, now you know how I came to be in Detroit attempting to sell my company to Mid-West Pork, a proposition that was accepted by the chairman of the company, with one caveat: the sale would include the contract to produce Krakus hams in Detroit, Michigan.

In fact, I had no control over the rights to the Krakus ham production in the United States; the Polish company that owned the Krakus label controlled them. This meant I had to get the Polish company to sign off on the deal. To do this, my American partner, Thomas Gardner of AKK, and I had to go to Poland to talk to the head of the Polish company and get his approval to transfer the Krakus ham production from Cherry Hill, New Jersey, to Detroit, Michigan. This was no easy task.

For one thing, the Polish company liked the way the Krakus hams were being produced in my plant and didn't want to change an operation that was a success, a sentiment that was echoed by Thomas on behalf of AKK.

Nonetheless, Thomas understood the financial struggle I had lived with for three years, and he reluctantly agreed to let me out of our partnership if the Polish company agreed to my proposal.

Working out the details of the trip with me over the phone, Thomas said: "Susan, I really wish things could stay as they are, but I understand your position. I'll accompany you to Warsaw to see Mr. Yeshenko, the chairman, but don't expect me to fight your battle for you. You'll have to do all the talking. I've had plenty of my own battles with him, and most of them had an unfavorable outcome."

"Thank you, Thomas. I look forward to traveling with you," I said, adding, "By the way, does Mr. Yeshenko speak English?"

"No," he said.

"Well, in that case, you'll have to translate for me," I said, knowing that Thomas had worked with the chairman for more than twenty years.

"I'm afraid you're on your own, Susan," he replied. "I don't speak Polish."

• • •

As we boarded the plane for Warsaw, I rated my odds of convincing Mr. Yeshenko at about a hundred to one. During the flight, I asked Thomas about the arrangements in Warsaw, but he was reticent, as if annoyed that he had agreed to accompany me. Nevertheless, I pressed him. "Tell me about the chairman's likes and dislikes," I said.

"I could never figure him out; he's a tough customer," Thomas said. "The only thing I can tell you for sure is that he likes Polish vodka . . . and I'm a teetotaler."

With that uplifting news, we made our descent into Warsaw. Scheduled to spend a day and a half, and two nights in Poland, we arrived the afternoon of the first day, whereupon Thomas left me on my own without a word of explanation.

It was a cold, gray day; a light drizzle misted the air. Poland felt unwelcoming as I checked in to the hotel and then walked the streets of Warsaw alone. A visit to the historic Warsaw Ghetto did nothing to lift my spirits.

Chilled to the bone, I returned to the hotel and went to the bar to see if I could get a crash course on Polish vodkas. I thought if I could learn a thing or two, I'd have at least one thing to discuss with the chairman, even if it was accomplished through hand gestures and head nods. Women are well suited to international business because they excel at developing strong relationships. For instance, they are likely to take an interest in local traditions to make others feel comfortable and accepted . . . in others words—actively connect by **being a perceptive communicator.**

The bartender spoke broken, but decent, English. After I explained my dilemma, he smiled, nodded, and poured five different Polish vodkas into shot glasses for me to taste. They left me dizzy and light-headed, but I still had enough wits about me to select vodka that actually went down easy. I had the bartender write the name on a paper napkin and tucked it into my purse.

"Can you give me some advice about drinking vodka with a powerful Polish company chairman? The truth is, I only drink vodka in Bloody Marys!"

The bartender chuckled. "We drink our vodka warm and straight up. We never add anything to it," he said. "If you want to make a friend of this powerful chairman, you'll need to follow our custom."

"Great," I said forlornly, "I'm a one-drink customer."

The bartender laughed. "Well, by tomorrow you better figure out how to keep up," he cautioned, "because the best way to show your chairman you can be trusted is to match him shot for shot."

My expression told the bartender this was never going to happen. So, together, we came up with a plan.

• • •

The next morning, I met Thomas in the hotel lobby at 7:30, and we took a ten-minute taxi ride to the headquarters of the Polish company. Our meeting wasn't scheduled for another two hours.

"Why are we here so early?" I asked.

"You'll see," is all he said.

We climbed three flights of stairs in the dingy, old gray building, which had formerly housed some of the Politburo in the communist days, and were met in the hallway by a stocky, bossy woman who appeared to be in charge. She spoke in Polish and, with hand gestures, indicated which way we should go. Ushering us down to the end of a hall, she then told us to line up single file against the wall. It was eight o'clock. We still had an hour and a half to wait.

"Now what?" I asked.

Thomas told me this was the old communist way. "We stand here until ten minutes before our appointed time and then we march down the hall and line up outside the chairman's door, so he doesn't have to wait for us. He's very punctual, and if we're not lined up outside his door when his assistant calls for us, our appointment is canceled."

"In that case," I said. "I'm taking off my high heels."

Time passed slowly in the cold, dark hallway. I reviewed in my head the information I would share with the chairman, and finally, at the designated time, I quickly put my high heels back on and we were marched down the hall. When we reached the chairman's office, we were motioned to enter.

The chairman, a short, bald, fair-skinned man of about fifty, greeted me with a faint smile when we shook hands. I sensed that he was impressed with the way my company had been able to duplicate the Krakus ham, and my instinct told me that this was a man who liked and appreciated women.

I was also convinced that the Polish ham–*meister* would have spoken well of me if he was ever asked. Paul and I had become very close friends. In fact, something about the chairman's almost warm initial greeting told me that perhaps he had already put in a good word for me.

After we were introduced, the chairman's interpreter turned to me and said, "Tell the chairman what you want."

I took out a recent financial statement of my ham company and handed it to the chairman. He studied it for a few moments then motioned for me to continue. I began by recounting the history of my ownership of the company, and the financial struggles that dogged me from day one. The interpreter translated as I explained why the company had already lost several million dollars, as he could see from the financial statements, and would probably not make any profit for at least several more years. I could see that the chairman was not one to sit by quietly and listen to a long, drawn-out recitation, so I got right to the point.

"Mr. Yeshenko," I said, "if your company and your American partner do not permit me to sell the company, I will file bankruptcy immediately and you will need to find someone to replace me."

I told him how he'd lose all the money his company had already put into this investment, but that if he allowed me to sell the equipment and inventory, and move the commitment to produce Krakus hams to the Detroit plant, his company and his American partner would make a 20 percent return on their initial investment at the time of the sale.

My knees were shaking a little when I delivered this bold ultimatum, but I needed to convey the urgency of my situation and let him know I was prepared to throw in the towel if he turned me down.

By this time, Thomas was visibly squirming in his seat, and Mr. Yeshenko's face had turned bright red. He turned to Thomas and, through his interpreter, asked him what he thought. I held my breath and tried not to shake.

"I support Susan's proposal," Thomas said.

After what seemed like an eternity of silence, Mr. Yeshenko said: "I will consider. We go for lunch."

It was ten o'clock in the morning. But the invitation wasn't a suggestion—it was a command.

We had left the building and had been walking for about five minutes when the chairman motioned for me to come alongside him, and together, we walked in silence for another minute or two. I got the impression the chairman was amused by the stares he got by having a confident, blonde, American woman walking beside him. I took it as a good sign when he reached for my arm, and we walked arm in arm down the street.

The restaurant provided a refreshing change from the somber office we'd just left. Everything was brightly decorated, and Polish music played in the background. None of the six or seven tables was occupied. The chairman sat down and motioned for me to sit next to him. Thomas and two other men from the chairman's office joined us. When the waiter came over, Mr. Yeshenko said to me: "I will order. Do you like vodka?"

"Yes," I said, taking out the napkin that I had put in my purse the night before and handing it to him.

He looked at it and let out a loud roar. *Like a mountain lion*, I thought. In English, he said to me, "This one is also my favorite!"

All smiles and warmth now, the chairman ordered two glasses of the vodka. After the first shot, I excused myself, saying I had to go to the ladies' room. What I was actually doing, though, was tracking down our waiter, as my friend the bartender had counseled. Finding him in the kitchen, I took out a wad of Polish money and asked him if he understood English. He said, *no*, but motioned for another, younger man to translate. Between the two of them, they were able to understand my request.

The waiter was skeptical, but he agreed to do what I was asking. After accepting the money, he made the sign of the cross.

I returned to the table and continued to match the chairman shot for shot six more times. After a typical Polish lunch, the chairman, now in a very good mood, gave me a discrete kiss on the cheek and said good-bye.

As we left the restaurant, Thomas told me the chairman would be back to us in a couple of days with his decision. He also told me that he'd never seen Mr. Yeshenko so amused and relaxed. Over the years, whenever he'd had serious discussions with the chairman and they disagreed, Mr. Yeshenko would get loud and belligerent. This day Thomas had witnessed a side of the chairman he'd not seen before.

To me, this was a clear indication of the power of a business*woman* at work. I was sure Mr. Yeshenko appreciated my direct approach ... not to mention the fact that I shared his love of Polish vodka!

Honest, straightforward, **perceptive communication**, combined with the **resourcefulness** to adapt to local customs, is how women get the job done in any language.

In the cab on the way back to the hotel, Thomas asked me how I could drink all that vodka. I never did tell him my secret, but the chairman approved the deal ... and no one was the wiser that my shots of the magnificent vodka had been diluted with water!

CHAPTER 11

Bandwagon Men

In chapter 8, you were introduced—perhaps not for the first time!—to female-phobic men and male bullies who, in one way or another, try to push women aside or intimidate them in the business world. The good news is that many male *mentors* also exist in that world, and these men sincerely support competent women in business by trying to help them, and even spread the word to others. Nurture your professional network by taking a page out of a businessman's book: practice building *transactional relationships*—those associations that occur as a result of business negotiations or interaction with customers, clients, supporters, mentors, and even companies that supply you with commodities.[1]

My supporter was a former banker responsible for promoting business in Vineland, New Jersey. After we met in 1996,

Jack Toretta and I developed a close business relationship that began during my negotiations with him to move my meat plant to Vineland. This transactional relationship grew into a much broader and mutually beneficial professional relationship and friendship that lasted for more than a decade. But let me back up a little.

Bragging Rights

When I bought Allied Steaks in 1987, I looked at the condition of the plant and opted not to buy the building—I leased it. So, by the end of 1996, my meat company was still renting plant space. With less than a year left on Allied's current lease, the property owner notified me he wasn't going to renew it.

Finding a USDA licensed plant at that time, in that area, and of the size I needed was a real challenge. After months of looking, and running out of time, I finally found a plant, but it was located almost fifty miles farther away than I had hoped—in Vineland, New Jersey.

But finding the property is just the first hurdle; financing it is the real challenge. I'd negotiated the purchase price for the property down from $1 million to $800,000, understanding that I'd still need to spend another $500,000 on improvements. This meant I needed to finance 80 percent or more of the purchase price to swing it.

I had no banking contacts in the area, so my initial strategy was to cold-call, in person, all the commercial banks in Vineland to try to secure a loan. I was discouraged to discover that although I'd been a successful businesswoman for more than ten years, not one of the banks was willing to give me even the courtesy of consideration.

The truth is, when it comes to borrowing from a bank, it's not just about your financial statements, it's also about your business relationships, and I realized I had none in Vineland.

Fortunately, that nexus was quickly filled when a banker who turned me down for a loan pointed me in an interesting direction. He told me that if I could bring new jobs to Vineland I might be able to get a loan from the Economic Development Authority in town. Although I'd never heard of the organization, I called and made an appointment with Jack Toretta, the director, and a former banker.

Jack's job was to bring new business to Vineland as part of a state and federal program to encourage new employment in the area, which had been designated an "economically disadvantaged" community.

From the time we met, Jack and I were fast friends. A truly personable guy, Jack was easily the most outgoing and gregarious banker I'd ever met—and a decision maker to boot. Plus, we had a prior connection: Jack had worked in a department of the local Philadelphia bank the Eagles had used during my tenure with them.

The more we talked, the more I was surprised to find out how much Jack knew about my travails with the Eagles . . . and not just the stuff that was in the papers. When I asked him how he knew so much of my history, he smiled and said, "Susan, the banking community is very tightly knit, and long before you and I met, our group at the bank would talk about what a tough spot you were in, especially for a woman."

I would have taken him to task for that *especially for a woman* comment if I thought he was putting me down. It was clear from the way he said it, however, that he was being sympathetic. And I quickly learned that Jack respected people who were straightforward, because that's the way he was, and if he believed you knew your business, it went a long way toward securing a loan from him.

I told Jack about the plant I wanted to buy; I also told him I could guarantee Vineland eighty new jobs, a prospect he jumped on enthusiastically. He told me to send him a brief outline about Allied and its needs, along with the past five years of my company's financial statements, and to come see him again the following week.

When we met again, I told Jack I needed to borrow the entire cost of the property—$800,000—and that my company would spend $500,000 during the first year to improve the property and build an addition.

At first he was hesitant, saying that it was too much for one project, and that he'd never loaned 100 percent of the real estate value to anyone.

But I was **persistent**. I dangled the jobs I'd bring to Vineland in his face every time we met, and I made sure he knew that Philadelphia wanted me to move there. It wasn't a contentious negotiation; it was good ol' horse-trading. There is no question that **being persistent** worked to my advantage: I convinced him to recommend that the Vineland Economic Development Authority provide 100 percent financing to purchase my new place.

Within a few weeks, thanks to Jack's emphatic recommendation, the proposal was accepted and I got my loan ... at the excellent rate (at the time) of just 4 percent.

This was a landmark moment in my career and a benchmark for all women in business. My banker was loaning me money on the same basis as his premier male customers. In other words, he was treating me as an equal, or even better, actually, because my mortgage was for the full purchase price of the building!

Sharing a mutual respect for each other, Jack and I worked well together in finding various ways to sell Vineland to other food companies that were looking to relocate.

What I call *quid pro quo*, other authors describe as "the art of reciprocity."[2] It's simply learning to understand, as I did, that Jack's hot button was bringing good jobs to Vineland, New Jersey. I enthusiastically agreed to conduct personal tours of my plant to any prospects that Jack identified. He seemed to take great pleasure in showcasing Allied *and me*, its owner.

Jack had found the ideal bragging rights to get other food companies to Vineland—a business that not only was successful but also had a woman owner. My plant became a regular stop on his guided tours, and I tacitly became a member of the "boy's business club" in Vineland by initiating and building a solid professional relationship with Jack Toretta.

(Note that not all business relationships are "transactional"—that is, arising out of doing a specific business deal together—but all of the ones women need to foster, including those that are transactional, are "professional" relationships even if they never do a business deal together.)

If you think **building professional relationships** is a piece of cake because we are great **communicators,** unfortunately you are mistaken. In this context women need lots of practice because although we are great at connecting with people, that does not translate automatically into **building professional relationships.**

Being a builder of professional relationships is the only place in this book where I suggest that you can learn something by observing how men do it. Men look at building relations by following their "hard-wired social instincts."[3] They have the ability to establish informal connections effortlessly; just consider all the activities men enjoy watching, or even playing occasionally, in a group: basketball, football, hockey, among many others. Unless you are sincerely a sports fan who understands the game you are watching, engaging in this activity will *not* give you an opportunity to build professional relationships.

BE #12   BEING A BUILDER OF PROFESSIONAL RELATIONSHIPS

Being a builder of professional relationships is a Briefcase Essential that takes considerable patience and practice. The most natural way to initiate your professional relationships is by expanding your contacts through business discussions and negotiations (transactional relationships) with buyers, customers, salespersons, clients, agents, and others that you meet while conducting business. Additionally, identify important business persons who you believe will be beneficial to you, and advance each relationship by going out of your way to offer something of value to the other business professional.[4]

The story that follows illustrates one of the ways in which I sustained my professional relationship with Jack Toretta by continuing to *practice* being a builder of professional relationships (BE #12).

A Colorful Encounter

Early one morning Jack called. "Susan, can you do a tour in thirty minutes?" he asked.

"Sure, how many people?" I replied.

"I don't know, but I'm sure you can handle it."

His evasive answer made me imagine, *Oh boy, large group!* But when he called back to confirm, I found out my imagination hadn't gone far enough.

"Susan, look out your window," he said. "A bus is coming down your street."

I immediately ran across the street to see if I could find enough white smocks and hats for everyone on the bus—who were practically on my doorstep by then. But what to wear wasn't the biggest issue of the day.

What Jack had failed to tell me was that the tourists were visiting from Japan . . . and no one in the group spoke a word of English!

As nearly forty men and women (mostly women) stepped off the bus, they each bowed low and smiled at my plant manager and me. Not knowing what else to do, I bowed back. Then I ushered them into the plant office to get them outfitted. They bowed low to every employee along the way.

I called Jack back. "I've been sandbagged!" I said.

Jack laughed. "I'm on my way, and I'm bringing someone who speaks Japanese," he said, much to my relief.

I quickly ran out of white smocks, but luckily, I had enough hats and smocks in various colors to outfit the whole group. When Jack arrived a little later, he burst into laughter at the sight of the forty Japanese visitors dressed in red, blue, yellow, white, and green coat and hat combinations, all bowing respectfully to my workers . . . who were covered in meat. It was like a wonderfully fanciful scene out of *Alice in Wonderland*.

He walked over to me and tapped me on the shoulder. "What's the matter, Susan? Didn't I loan you enough money to buy more than a few coats in each color?" he asked jokingly.

"Jack, I just wanted to make my meat plant the most colorful one in Vineland," I said.

To which he replied, "Susan, with you as its owner, it already is."

The tour lasted about an hour and a half—about half an hour longer than usual because, as the visitors left, each repeated their customary bow to each worker in the plant. Although my company was much less productive on tour days, I recognized the intangible value that I was providing to Vineland and the value that my company received in return.

A few minutes later, as Jack was driving away, he shouted out to me, "I owe you one!"

"Don't worry," I yelled back. "I'll collect!"

I understood at that moment that my personal involvement—that is, a woman's touch—had made the tour *memorable* to everyone—something Jack had figured out long before me.

Jack-too

Another Jack played a big part in helping me succeed . . . when it came time to sell Allied. I'll call him Jack-too because, as much as I'd like to tell you his last name, the truth is, I never knew it. In fact, I never met him. All of our communication was over the phone.

Jack-too was the production manager of a McDonald's plant in Athens, Georgia. We "met" when McDonald's contracted with my company to develop a Philly steak for them, using *flash freezing*. This technique, developed by my company, involved freezing every slice of meat very quickly just prior to packaging, and no one else in the industry at the time had figured out how to duplicate it.

The deal was this: After Allied successfully produced the initial one million pounds of steak, our staff would work with the McDonald's production team to teach them our process. Steak production would then be transferred to the McDonald's plant.

Normally, an owner would delegate this training job to the plant manager because the owner would not generally know the technical details—in this case, about nitrogen freezing, slicing temperatures, and process flow. And even if they knew the information, most owners (who were generally men) would not want to spend hours a day for several months tied up on the phone with another company's plant manager.

Women business owners, however, are much more *hands on* than men are. Because McDonald's was a huge, valuable customer, I wanted the transfer of the business to McDonald's to go off without a hitch, and they wanted my personal assurance that it would. Therefore, I personally handled all of the discussions with the plant manager.

The roles of trainer and trainee were switched in the instance of Jack-too: he was asking all the questions, and I was providing all the answers. Generally, men ask fewer questions than women do because men believe that asking questions means they are asking for help, and at the same time, they feel that this indicates a reduced decision-making status.[5] Jack-too was the exception because he knew he needed help and I owned the company. This enabled Jack-too and I to develop a meaningful professional relationship.

This brings up another important question: How does a woman tell a man what she knows?

The simple answer is *carefully*—by **being a perceptive communicator**—in a way that doesn't embarrass him or damage his credibility in the eyes of others. Businesswomen understand that the best way to build trust and friendship is to avoid snitching and backstabbing just to show how much you know about a subject.

For several months, I worked with Jack-too over the phone to get him up and running, and it was clear from the start that there was a lot about the process he didn't understand. I patiently answered each and every question without ever being patronizing, condescending, or telling his superiors that Jack-too had limited production knowledge.

Jack-too came to rely on me as his production adviser, and I made sure his superiors never knew the depth and breadth of the questions he asked and the knowledge I passed on to him. A woman in business builds relationships by offering something of value and *not* telling tales out of school.

When the big bosses from McDonald's visited my plant, they'd grill me on how Jack-too was doing, always impatient with his progress. My honest answer was the same every time: "Jack is very talented and motivated, and if I needed a plant manager, I'd hire him in a minute."

Although I was the owner of the company and Jack-too was not in an executive position at McDonald's (and despite the fact that I was in New Jersey and he was in Georgia), he and I developed an excellent, trusting working relationship because of the mutual respect we showed each other. When you make an honest effort to establish a valuable *transactional relationship* that benefits the other person significantly more than it does you—as I did with Jack-too—the benefit will eventually come back to you.

Once production was fully transferred to Georgia, I had no further communication with Jack-too until . . . one day, about six months later, when he called me out of the blue.

"Susan," he said, "would you be interested in selling your company?"

His call definitely caught me off guard, but not for the reasons you might think.

About six months before I'd ever spoken to Jack, I'd decided that, after twenty years in the meat business, it was time to sell my company and move on. I'd even hired a prominent mergers and acquisitions firm to help me find a buyer. But, after spending thousands of dollars and almost a year looking, I was no closer to selling my business than before I started. The only prospects the firm came up with wanted to strip the company— the same way the company in Detroit had stripped Suzannah Farms—and move the plant out of New Jersey.

Women have different priorities than men do when selling a business. The reasons I turned down prior offers from others to buy Allied (which businessmen would consider immaterial) were based on the *human* and *community* aspects of business.[6]

First, I was not going to leave my employees in the lurch; I made a promise after closing my ham plant never to shut down another plant, and I intended to keep it. Second, I felt a commitment was owed to the town itself, and to Jack Toretta, to keep Allied in Vineland. The community had bent over backwards to finance my move there, and loaned me additional money through the years, and at least half of my employees lived in Vineland and would be out of work if I shut down the plant.

Women consider all of these factors before selling a business. I was just listening to my gut and the values, shared by most women, that by sustaining cultures, we enhance the lives of both employees and communities.[7]

Because I could not find a buyer who met my first two priorities, I had all but given up on selling the company . . . when Jack-too called.

I'd never told Jack-too of my plans to sell the company. But when someone he had worked for in Chicago was looking to buy a few successful boutique meat businesses and contacted him, Jack-too immediately thought of me. That's how *quid pro quo* works: I hadn't expected anything in return for helping Jack-too, but he had returned the favor! If I had delegated working with Jack to my plant manager, this opportunity would never have happened.

I thanked Jack-too and told him I'd be happy to speak with his former boss. A phone call to this potential buyer led to a more than satisfactory agreement: the plant and the jobs would be kept in Vineland, and I'd receive a selling price that was 500 percent more than what I'd paid for Allied in 1987.

On my last day as company owner, my employees threw a going-away party for me. As they took turns coming into the cafeteria to say good-bye, we shared hugs and reminiscences. Just before I left, they presented me with a wonderful framed photograph of me with many of my employees standing in front of the plant.

That night, I drove home with a heavy heart, but no regrets. I'd kept my promise to my employees to keep the Vineland plant going, and the almost twenty years I'd spent working at my meat company were filled with priceless human lessons learned about the benefits of working in your own business.

My head was also swimming with ideas for my next venture, and by the time I got home, I had focused on the opportunity that I intended to pursue. Within a week, I secured a commitment from a former supplier to sell their fresh beef products.

I was back in business!

CHAPTER 12

A Wild and Wooly Ride

Choosing to become a business owner may not be every woman's cup of tea. It's a wild and wooly ride on a roller coaster that's full of bumps and turns, stops and starts, and sometimes even makes you sick. But I highly recommend it!

I urge you to always leave open the possibility of being in business for yourself. You do not need a bunch of fancy degrees or special skills. Just bring the innate abilities that have been identified in this book as Briefcase Essentials and use them wisely. Yes, owning a business means the buck stops with you, but that's a good thing because, on the flip side, you control your own destiny and call the shots. If you have children, it will give you the opportunity to carve out a flexible schedule without your boss looking at the clock when you leave early.

Women are leading the way as entrepreneurs by starting a business every *sixty seconds*.[1] And, as if that isn't impressive enough, women also own the majority interest in 10.4 million privately held businesses. That's approximately 40 percent of *all* privately held firms in the United States.[2] The astounding number of successful women-owned businesses is a testament to the fact that this option is wide open and available—if you are ready to get your feet wet.

Unfortunately, women are losing ground in reaching top positions at large public corporations, where only 2 percent of Fortune 500 CEOs are women and only 15 percent of the seats on boards of directors are held by women.[3] According to the authors of *Enlightened Power*, "Every day, an average of 1,400 to 1,600 women leaders are leaving *Fortune 500* companies to start their own businesses or work for competitors—twice the rate of their male counterparts."[4]

These numbers are exhilarating if you are contemplating starting or buying your own business, but disheartening if you are headed to work for a large public corporation.

Of course, you don't have to *own* a business or work in corporate America in order to succeed. Thousands of other business opportunities are out there just waiting for you to walk in the door and make your mark. Regardless of which business path you choose, by learning, practicing, and committing to use these twelve Briefcase Essentials—*all* day, *every* day—you will achieve success in any workplace, even if it's one that is dominated by males.

A View That Never Gets Old

The greatest advantage you have as a woman in the world of business, and in the world, is that being a woman is part and parcel of what makes you tick. I've stated this often throughout this book because it's always worth remembering that women are unique. We're different from men, and that's a good thing!

It's true that women in business often find themselves in a good ol' boys club environment, filled mostly by men, which is both intimidating and exclusive ... much like what a woman might experience in a men's locker room. Just in case you've never been there, this final story (my favorite) explains why I went into a business of my own choosing after working for the Philadelphia Eagles. I've been there, done that, and discovered that once was probably enough!

The Locker Room

Back when I was the VP and acting general manager of the Eagles, I had a front-row seat to observe some of the greatest male physiques in the world. My office was in the hallway with the coaches' offices, and right next to the office of the head coach. During the football season, I had the distinct pleasure of seeing a steady procession of young, strong, incredibly well-built professional football players—wearing nothing more than tight-fitting athletic shorts and T-shirts—stroll by my office.

Part of my job was to negotiate players' contracts, so I was often in close contact with them, but their obvious attractiveness notwithstanding, my interaction with them was always completely professional. In fact, I probably appeared more than a little standoffish. After three years of watching the scantily clad players parade up and down the hall, it was definitely ho-hum.

One day, the Eagles' head trainer, Barney Howard, called me on the phone. He was a tough, hard-nosed, no-nonsense man in his mid-fifties, nearly six feet tall and built like an army tank. Barney had been a trainer all his life and spoke with a slow West Texas drawl. On the surface, he appeared to have the bluster of a male chauvinist, but nothing could have been further from the truth. In fact, Barney and I were good friends, and I valued his opinion.

A bit of advice is in order here: Don't be afraid to let men surprise you; you never know who is going to turn out to be your ally.

So, I got this call from Barney to come to his office. As I was in charge of the Eagles budget, I had approved the purchase of some expensive equipment to help speed the rehabilitation of players with serious muscular injuries.

"The machines are here, Susan," Barney said over the phone. "I'd like you to come down and look them over."

"Thanks, Barney. I'll be right down. Just tell me where your office is," I said, never having been there before.

"It's in the basement, directly behind the players' locker room," he said. "Just go through the locker room and you'll come right to it."

The locker room was another place I'd never been. I felt it was the players' inner sanctum, a *no-woman's-land* where I just didn't belong. But, as this was the off-season, and Barney directed me through it, I assumed it would be deserted.

The basement was dimly lit and quiet when I stepped off the elevator, and after making a turn or two down the hall, I reached the locker room. Expecting it to be empty, I opened the door . . . and was shocked to see five huge players standing there stark naked, dripping water on the locker room floor, an obvious indication that they had just left the shower room after a workout. Equally startled to see me, they quickly grabbed their towels.

My first instinct was to turn and run out of the room screaming . . . but instead, I took a deep breath and stepped audaciously into the brightly lit room, hoping for some brilliant one-liner to pop into my head and out of my mouth. But it was one of the players, an all-pro cornerback, who broke the silence.

"Guys," he said, "on *three*, drop your towels. One . . . two . . ."

On three, down went the towels, and there they stood, naked as the day they were born, and smiling proudly.

Naked as they were, they couldn't have possibly felt as exposed as I did at that moment. I knew I was being baited, and although I was trembling inside, I refused to be intimidated and was determined not to show my embarrassment.

Gathering my wits, I moved closer to the all-pro cornerback until we were almost toe-to-toe. Slowly, deliberately, I looked him up and down, lingering on the important parts of his anatomy.

Then I turned and started toward Barney's office . . . but looked back briefly, shrugged my shoulders, and shouted, "Big deal!"

Fortunately, self-preservation took over, and I left the locker room outwardly appearing to maintain the same confident demeanor I carried with me when I'd left the two Tonys in the principal's office fifteen years earlier. And the hysterical laughing of the football players as they razzed their abashed teammate reminded me of Tony senior's laughing at his son that day.

Being able to stand my ground by teasing the admittedly well-endowed player in the Eagles' locker room, I was pretending that what had just happened wasn't a big deal at all . . . but we both knew it really was.

Barney knew it too. Once inside his office, I told him what happened, and he almost fell over laughing. When he saw the frown on my face, he said: "Look, what do you expect? You're the boss's daughter; you work for a professional football team. You think they would've done that if they *didn't* like you?"

• • •

About five months later, when the football season started, we were boarding the bus to ride back to the airport after the first away game. The all-pro cornerback had taken his time getting out of the locker room. When he finally boarded the bus, one of the other players shouted out, "Hey, Big Deal, what took you so long?"

Sitting in the front row of the bus, I chuckled to myself. Until that moment, I'd had uneasy feelings about the locker room incident, but once I heard the nickname I gave the player repeated by one of his buddies, I realized that I had handled the locker room incident just right. But it was only years later that I could laugh about it.

• • •

A final word on how to succeed in business . . . well, two words: *honesty* and *humor*.

Be honest with others, and above all, be honest with yourself. What I've found in all my years in business is that if you're honest, every success is exhilarating, because you know you've done the best you can do, without cutting corners and without cheating others. And when, even with the most honest effort, success is elusive, you'll feel good about the effort and the lessons learned, valuable lessons you can take to your next opportunity.

Which brings us to humor. In business, as in life, you'll need it. As you have seen in many of the experiences I've shared in this book, I've used humor to accomplish my goals, to make others feel good, and to make myself feel better about things that were not so good, even if only in hindsight.

• • •

So, keep a copy of *Briefcase Essentials* with you to refer to now and again so that you can remember what you have "discovered"—twelve *proven business essentials* for you to rely on that complement your natural talents and values. Trust your natural talents to pull you through regardless of the workplace . . . and you *will* succeed.

I leave you with these words (attributed to Groucho Marx) that capture the essence of this book:

"ONLY ONE MAN IN A THOUSAND IS A LEADER OF MEN—THE OTHER 999 FOLLOW WOMEN."[5]

Briefcase Essentials will help *you* be one of those women.

NOTES

CHAPTER 1 TENNIS ANYONE?

1. Helen E. Fisher, *The First Sex* (New York: Ballantine Books, 2000), 87.
2. Ibid.
3. Ibid., 84.
4. Margaret Heffernan, *How She Does It* (New York: Penguin Group, 2007), 239.
5. Ibid.
6. Alice. E. Eagly, and Linda L. Carli, *Through the Labyrinth* (Boston: Harvard Business School Press, 2007), 191.

CHAPTER 2 PAPILLON SPREADS ITS WINGS

1. Joanna Barsh, and Susie Cranston, *How Remarkable Women Lead* (New York: Crown Business, 2005), 77, 112.

CHAPTER 3   THE EAGLES HAVE LANDED . . . AT MY FEET

1. Heffernan, 191.
2. Ibid., 180–193.
3. Ibid., 239.

CHAPTER 4   PRESENTATION, PRESENTATION, PRESENTATION

1. Barsh, 187–189.

CHAPTER 5   OUT OF THE FRYING PAN, INTO THE FIRE

1. Sally Helgesen, *The Female Advantage* (New York: Doubleday, 1995), 27.
2. Heffernan, 30–31. See also Barsh, 139–142.
3. Fisher, 16–17.
4. Barsh, 134–135, 182, 194. See also Linda Coughlin, Ellen Wingard, and Keith Hollihan, *Enlightened Power* (San Francisco: Jossey-Bass, 2005), 13–14, 434–436; and Linda Tarr-Whelan, *Women Lead the Way* (San Francisco: Berrett-Koehler, 2009), 80.
5. Coughlin, 328.
6. Heffernan, 129.

CHAPTER 6   BUYING A PIG IN A POKE

1. http://www.alfsv.org/index.php?src=gendocs&ref= JohnWGardnerLeadershipAward&category=Programs.
2. Heffernan, 30.
3. Ibid., 10–15.
4. Ibid., 70.
5. Ibid., citing David Sirota, Louis A. Mischkind, and Michael I. Meltzer, *The Enthusiastic Employee: How Companies Profit by Giving Workers What They Want* (Wharton School Publishing, 2005).

CHAPTER 7 THE DEVIL IS IN THE DETAILS

1. Barsh, 223.

CHAPTER 9 THERE'S NO CRYING IN BUSINESS ... OR IS THERE?

1. Fisher, 5.
2. Heffernan, 86–90.
3. Simon Baron-Cohen, *The Essential Difference* (New York: Basic Books, 2004), 1–60.
4. Ibid., 60.
5. Ibid., 23.

CHAPTER 10 ANOTHER GREAT OPPORTUNITY

1. Fisher, 84.
2. Ibid.
3. Eagly, 144.

CHAPTER 11 BANDWAGON MEN

1. Barsh, 129–130.
2. Ibid., 128.
3. Ibid., 143.
4. Ibid., 143–152.
5. Fisher, 35.
6. Coughlin, 228.
7. Heffernan, 92.

CHAPTER 12 A WILD AND WOOLY RIDE

1. Marie C. Wilson, *Closing the Leadership Gap* (New York: Penguin Books, 2007), 3.
2. Eagly, 19–20.

3. Ibid., 19.
4. Coughlin, 7–8.
5. http://en.wikiquote.org/wiki/Talk:Groucho_Marx.

ABOUT THE AUTHOR

Susan T. Spencer graduated with honors and awards from Boston University and Villanova Law School, and she also received an MA in history/economics from Hofstra—where her thesis on "The Role of Women in Business During the Revolutionary War, 1770–1785" provided no small bit of foreshadowing of all her own achievements to come.

After stints as a junior high school history teacher, a corporate lawyer, and starting a successful tennis clothes company (Papillon) that sold to Neiman Marcus and Saks Fifth Avenue, she decided to throw herself headfirst into the far-flung, high stakes, male-dominant world of business.

Her first stop was none other than an NFL franchise, the Philadelphia Eagles, where from 1980 to 1985 she served as vice president, legal counsel, and acting general manager (the team went to its first Super Bowl under her watch in 1981). Never to be intimidated by rowdy Eagles fans or locker room antics, Susan is the only woman ever to hold this trifecta of positions in NFL history.

And when the team was sold, whereas most people might use that kind of clout and leadership to segue into a vague but fanciful consulting job, Susan went directly into one of the dirtiest, bloodiest, male-dominated industries there is: meat.

Myriad skills are necessary to successfully own and run a meat processing and distribution business: strong leadership, negotiating savvy, the ability to win and maintain the loyalty of your workers, the willingness to make difficult decisions regarding plant closings, cash flow, personnel, etc., to name just a few. And while most of these attributes would traditionally be associated almost exclusively with the male gender (one reason why Susan was one of the few women running businesses in the meat industry in America during this time), she not only chose to build her life within this industry but also loved doing it. From 1986 to the present, the results speak for themselves.

She took Allegro Foods (Atlantic City) from a start-up food distributor to $10 million in sales—in the span of just three years.

As owner of another meat processing company, Allied Steaks, she increased sales tenfold, from $2 million to $20 million, during her tenure (and was the only female meat supplier to such fast food and casual restaurants as McDonald's, Jack in the Box, Chili's, and many others).

She brought the world-famous Krakus ham brand from Poland and processed Krakus hams in the United States for the first time, to the tune of $40 million in sales, before selling her company, Suzannah Farms, to one of the largest ham producers in this country.

Most recently, in addition to being an author and speaker and recipient of numerous women's business awards, she has launched her own meat commodities trading company, ASCM, and is teaching **Briefcase Essentials** to a group of high-school-age girls under a program sponsored by the Nevada Girl Scouts.

Susan likewise is guest lecturing about starting your own business to undergraduates and students in the MBA program at UNLV. She has also started a lecture series with health-care professionals in Nevada, with special emphasis on empathy and compassion as they relate to credibility in the business world.

For more than twenty years, as a woman in a "man's world," Susan Spencer has led in an unconventional way by ignoring every single "No High Heels Allowed" sign she encountered along the way. And though it might seem logical that in order to do so she must have had to use skills that enable many men to excel in business, her triumphs came, in fact, from recognizing and developing certain natural talents and skills that most women possess, and taking away lots of lessons from her experiences.